The Face of the Waters

Eliezer Shore

The Face of the Waters
CHASIDIC TEACHINGS AND STORIES FOR THE TWENTY-FIRST CENTURY

TEHIRU PRESS

Copyright © 2017 Eliezer Shore

All rights reserved. No part of the text may be reproduced in any form, nor may any page be photographed and reproduced by any means, without the written permission of the publisher.

Set in ITC Legacy by Raphaël Freeman, Renana Typesetting
Cover design: Yael Knochen
Questions and comments can be sent to tehirupress@gmail.com

ISBN: 978-1-56871-623-7

*In the beginning,
God created the heaven and the earth.
And the earth was without form and void;
and darkness was on the surface of the deep.
And the spirit of God moved
across the face of the waters.*
GENESIS 1

There is no "water" other than Torah.
MEGILLAH 21B

Dedicated to the Loving Memory of

Moshe and Leah Assor

By their daughter

Tovah Assor

תנצב"ה

לעילוי נשמת

משה בן הרב בנימין עשור

ולאה בת הרב יהודה אלקובי

ובת מורת אסתר טולדנו

מגוע חכמי ורבני מרוקו

נתרם על ידי בתם

טובה עשור הי"ו

תנצב"ה

Contents

Some Background	xi
An Invocation	1
Immanence	3
The Soul of Community	5
Among Breslover Chasidim	12
Discipline	17
A New Song	19
Heart of Stone	25
The Power of Prayer	27
Consciousness	31
At the Center	33
Neighbors	39
The Soul	43
Through a Dark Passage	45
The Paper Piano	50
The Penny Candle	57
Integration	61
The Milk of Miracles	63
The Maggid's Coin	68
Goals	79
Seeds of Vision	81
Counting Back the Minutes	88
The Midnight Ride	90

Faith	97
Dweller on the Plain	99
Simchas Torah of the Chazon Ish	105
The Souvenir	107
Compassion	113
Writing Between the Lines	115
Black Fire on White Fire	122
The First Lesson	127
Returning	131
The Still Small Voice	133
The Troops of God	141
The Heart	149
Solomon's Dream	151
A Change of Clothing	157
Relationships	159
Standing Beneath the Mountain	161
The Essence of Study	167
Slim	168
Song of the Shepherds	177
Changes	181
The Temple of Amount	183
The Untouched Oil	192
Responsibility	201
The Age of Tikkun	203
A Single Glance	209
Glossary	217
Biographies	223
Notes and Sources	229

Some Background

My interest in and commitment to Torah was not always like it is today. I grew up in a secular Jewish home, with little Jewish knowledge or education, and even the little I did receive did not continue much past my bar-mitzvah. My main interests were music, film, and theater, which I went to college to study.

Yet, in 1980, at the age of twenty and in the middle of my junior year, I felt an irrepressible urge to leave school and explore the world. I spent most of the following year trekking across the moors and mountains of Northern England and Scotland, and then living in an abandoned cabin in the Blue Ridge Mountains of North Carolina. My reading during this period was mostly comprised of books on Buddhism, Taoism, and Native America spirituality, and my time was largely spent walking in the woods and contemplating life's meaning.

On returning to school in the middle of 1981, I changed my major to religious studies. I continued in an Eastward direction until graduation, studying Japanese, and practicing Zen meditation, Kung Fu, and wilderness survival. I participated in several silent retreats, and fully expected to enter a Buddhist monastery after graduation in 1982.

Unexpectedly, as part of a religious studies class that

I took in my final semester, I met Rabbi Dovid Din – an important figure in the early *ba'al teshuvah* movement in America. Reb Dovid, as we called him, was a brilliant and charismatic teacher. More than that, he was a genuine mystic, who knew how to enter deep states of meditation and self-transcendence. There is a famous saying among spiritual searchers: "When the student is ready, the teacher appears" – and it truly applied to me at that moment. However, "the teacher" came with a twist; for everything I had been searching for – all the depth and profundity I had found in Eastern religions – I now heard from Reb Dovid, a Chasidic Jew. I was drawn to his teachings and personality, as much as I was terrified and repulsed by them – for they demanded commitment to a path that meant major changes in my life and goals. After a long inner struggle, I gave up my Buddhist identity and accepted my Jewish one, reconnecting to the tradition in which I had been born, though had never offered me any meaningful values during my childhood.

For four years after graduation, I was Reb Dovid's assistant and secretary, and perhaps his closest student. Even now, thirty years after his passing, his influence on my life is still strong. Reb Dovid taught me how to learn Torah, how to understand Chasidus, how to take the ideas of Judaism and Kabbalah and apply them to the broadest possible framework, bringing the light and life of Divinity to the entire world, and into one's private life

Eventually, I moved on – physically, from Brooklyn to Jerusalem, and intellectually, learning from other books and teachers; however, the message of those early years has never left me. It is the idea that Torah has something significant to say about life itself, that Judaism is not just a religion or a matter of keeping *mitzvos*, observing Shabbos or studying

Torah, but a path that embraces all of life, and in doing so, brings a deeper and profounder understanding and appreciation to life itself. *Chazal* say: "The Torah speaks in the language of man" (*Berachos* 31b), which I understand to mean that the Torah has something to say to every person, in the language of his or her generation, addressing all his dreams and concerns.

Thus, this world is never rejected or abandoned, but embraced and uplifted. This applies to each person and to every system of knowledge. It was clearly embodied by Reb Dovid in his lectures and teachings – which often included discussions of philosophy, psychology, history and comparative religion – in his vast library of books on every possible topic, and in his regular dialogues with spiritual leaders from different religious traditions. It is how I understand that path of the Baal Shem Tov, and how I try to live my own life, as well – navigating between the poles of holiness and piety on the one hand, and openness and universality, on the other.

The essays and stories in this book are the fruit of over twenty years of thinking and writing about these things from my own perspective. They reflect the struggles and challenges that are born out of the encounter of the ancient with the contemporary, the holy and the mundane, the drive for single-minded spiritual pursuit and the desire to find God everywhere, at all times. Most of the essays were written for *Parabola* Magazine, a quarterly publication dedicated to "Tradition, Myth and the Search for Meaning," though a number of unpublished pieces appear here, as well. Many of these essays appeared at one point in *Bas Ayin*, a small journal of Jewish spirituality that I published from 1991 to 1998. The stories (which I began writing in 1992, after taking a class with famed American Jewish storyteller, Peninnah Schram) were mostly written for *Bas Ayin*, although some of them appeared afterward in various anthologies. Some are true stories, which I witnessed myself, some are retellings of tales I have read (usually in Hebrew), and a few are original. There are two pieces here that I did not write. The first is a translation of a description of a Breslover Shul in Berditchev. It was written by Rabbi Hillel Zeitlin - a great writer on Chasidus before World War II. The piece was translated by my dear friends, Rabbi Dovid Sears and Rabbi Dovid Zeitlin, and appeared in *Bas Ayin*, Issue 1. The second story, "Black Fire on White Fire," was written by a friend of mine, Rabbi Yehoshua Rubin, and first appeared in *Bas Ayin*, Issue 12. Both pieces are beautiful, and I could not resist including them here, especially as each complements the article before it.

For the most part, when I originally wrote these essays, I did not include the primary sources that I had in mind at the time; though, in assembling this volume, I tried to locate as many of these sources as I could. You will find them at the end of the book. The list is not exhaustive, but is meant to illustrate that these ideas, while dressed in new garments, are solidly based on classic Chasidic thought. Reb Dovid first introduced me to Breslover Chasidus, and it has always been a strong influence in my life and my approach to Torah. Besides Rabbi Nachman, I have spent a good deal of time studying many different Chasidic thinkers, although the greatest influence on my thought have been the writings of Rabbi Tzadok HaKohen of Lublin. More recently, I have gained great knowledge from the teachings of Rabbi Mordechai Zilber of Stutchin, *shlit"a* - a leading Chasidic thinker in Brooklyn, New York. And always, I find deep inspiration in

Some Background

the teachings of the Baal Shem Tov, the founder of Chasidus. His openness to the world and the fearlessness that allows him to find God everywhere lies at the heart of my Judaism.

This is not a book to read in one sitting, but rather, to dip into on occasion, for an interesting or inspiring essay or tale. I have tried to arrange the essays and stories in a way that complement each other, and have added, before each essay, some of the thoughts and experiences that originally inspired me to write it. There are also quotations along the way from Chasidic masters. It isn't meant to be digested all at once. I hope, however, that you will enjoy all its contents.

There are many people who deserve mention and thanks for the love and support they have given me over the many years of my searching – too many individuals to be named here. Still, a few deserve special mention. My wife, Devorah, for her love, sacrifice and patience, which allows me to do that which I feel most called to. My parents, for years of unqualified support and appreciation. My incredible children: Yoni, Ariel, Elisha, Adina and Kayla. And many of my good friends, with whom I have shared hours of conversation, whether about Torah or about life. Among them: Dovid Sears, Simcha Betten, Dovid Gross, Moshe Mykoff, Shlomo Aharon Gottlieb, Baruch Gartner, Eliezer Vogel, Benyamin Adilman, Yehoshua Leavitt, Moshe Genuth, and Sarah Yehudit Schneider, to name just a few. A special thanks to Tovah Assor, who sponsored the first printing of this book in memory of her dear parents, Moshe and Leah Assor.

In conclusion, I would like to dedicate this book to my beloved friend and teacher, Rabbi Dovid Din, may his memory be a blessing.

An Invocation

Where does the sacred dwell? It dwells in those things beyond our grasp, beyond our power to manipulate or control – a selfless deed, a silent prayer, a star-filled night. It lies in those things that cannot be reduced to our personal concerns, but rather, lift us up, inspire us, and serve as a doorway to a vision greater and more perfect than our own.

What makes a human being sacred? It is the part of each person that can never be touched, that exists in this world independent of me, an essence that will always remain beyond. For in grasping it, I grasp only its shell; in defining it, I limit only myself. But when I recognize the uniqueness of the other, when I cease to regard a human being as a mere object in my life, but remember that he or she is the center of his own world, as true and as complete as my own, then I sanctify and uplift the other, and they become a doorway to a world higher and more noble than mine.

How do we build a world that is sacred? When we no longer regard its creatures solely in terms of our needs, to use or abuse. When we treat each thing with respect, allowing it time and space to grow. When we remember that all things have a greater purpose in the service of God. Then creation becomes a doorway to the fullness of being, and a life in the service of the Holy One.

May it be the will of the One who is totally beyond, yet who dwells in the heart of every human being, to open our hearts to all that is sacred in this world, in ourselves and in others. May we help each creature find and fulfill its purpose in life, and in doing so, may we see the Divinity in all things. And so, may we pass through the doorway into the holy sanctuary of the world.

IMMANENCE

*Let them make Me a sanctuary,
that I may dwell among them.*

– Exodus 25:8

I REMEMBER WALKING DOWN THE STREETS OF Manhattan, in the months after graduating from college, and considering the possibility of entering a Buddhist monastery. The temptation was great and there were some wonderful options available. One thought held me back, however. If God really existed, then it should be possible to find Him everywhere – not necessarily in a monastery or the mountains of Tibet, but even on the streets of New York. Later, I came to understand that for Chasidus, this is indeed the goal.

The Soul of Community

Several times in my life I have tried to escape the everyday world. In mountain huts, on ocean bluffs, in the still predawn hours, I sought a truth that I could not find among friends. Yet there was always something missing, something incomplete that kept calling me back.

Several times in my life I have tried to enter the world – with community projects, group discussions, the routines of family and workplace. But I was always pulled back. Something was missing, an inner point that was not being addressed.

Most spiritual seekers, at some time in their journey, must struggle with the dilemma posed by these opposites. While personalities differ, some tending towards solitude, others to community, most of us waver uneasily between the two, constantly searching for the proper balance with which we might best serve God. In the midst of joyous community celebration, a small voice can make itself heard, whispering in the pause between speeches, reminding us that there is something more. And in a quiet forest glen, a peculiar loneliness echoes through the woods, calling us back to the world, to share our discoveries with others.

The greatness of community is that it provides us with a context for our lives. Before we can know God, we must come to know ourselves. Without a sense of identity, a person cannot be whole; it is community that gives a person his name. Social relationships, responsibilities, larger values, all help us know who we are. In an ideal community, each person's place would be so clearly defined as to make him indispensable. This engenders a sort of horizontal growth, as our lives touch and are touched by many others, and it fosters in us a greater compassion and awareness of the human condition. In Judaism, we find the ultimate curse to be that of exile, the dispersion of community, the loss of one's place.

On the other hand, solitude speaks to the part of us that has no name, that wants to break free of the limitations imposed upon us by the thoughts and expectations of others. Solitude holds the promise of such complete and utter commitment to God – such pure vertical growth – that one completely transcends the mundane concerns of this world and moves into a realm of pure spirit. There, everything is good, everything is holy, and God alone is real. "Abraham was one," say the verse (Ezekiel 33:24). Like our father Abraham, a person who wants only God must learn to be one and alone.

The validity of both these positions, and the pull they exert on our lives, stems from the fact that solitude and community are two necessary components in the metaphysical makeup of man, based upon the interplay of body and soul. Community is a function of the body. Not only because the body has needs that can only be met by the community; Judaism understands that physical needs, and even emotional ones, are products of man's corporeality. The body, as a composite entity, intrinsically relates to the "body of the community," with its integration and interrelation of parts.

The Soul of Community

In Chasidic writings, the community is often referred to in physical terms. The head of the community is its leaders; the heart, its poets and dreamers; the hands, its workers; the legs and feet, its financial supporters. Every single element is necessary, for if even one is missing, it causes a defect in the entire communal body.

Solitude, however, is the domain of the soul. Kabbalah understands the soul to be a portion of God Himself. As such, it shares in His total and unique Oneness and Transcendence. The soul does not need this world, and God must force it to remain in the body, for it cannot bear limitation. Chasidic writings often compare the soul to a flame, burning with a constant love and awe of God, seeking at every moment to rise upward and be reabsorbed in its source. "The soul of man is a candle of God, searching out all the chambers of the heart" (Proverbs 20:27). It is precisely in solitude that soul feels most at home, in a setting closest to its own essential nature.

Solitude has always been an important aspect of Jewish spirituality. Inherent in the Biblical image of the Patriarchs as shepherds is the idea that these men were contemplatives seeking a truth beyond the false gods of society. Throughout Jewish history, and especially in the lives of the great mystics, solitude has played an important role. The great sixteenth-century Kabbalist, Rabbi Yitzchok Luria, spent seven years in a hut on the Nile contemplating the mysteries of the Zohar, the Kabbalistic Book of Splendor. The Baal Shem Tov developed the path of Chasidus during his years of solitude in the Carpathian Mountains. His great-grandson, the famous Rabbi Nachman of Breslov, went so far as to say that one hour of solitude a day is a religious obligation as important as the formal daily prayers.

Nonetheless, even the great mystics eventually put aside their solitary endeavors to reunite with the community – Rabbi Yitzhak Luria became the leader of the holy community of Kabbalists in Safed in Northern Israel, and the Chasidic movement of the Baal Shem Tov was eminently communal. This is because the path of Judaism, while recognizing the need for solitude, clearly emphasizes the primacy of community as a vehicle for the revelation of God and the transformation of the world.

From its very inception as a nation – the deliverance from Egypt and the group revelation of God at Mount Sinai – community has been the focus and backbone of the Jewish nation. The Torah, including both the Bible and the Talmud, is by and large, a testament of communal spirituality. In this, it is something of a holy constitution, whose main concern is to reveal God's presence in the mundane aspects of life. It speaks of business and finance, agriculture, family relations, and national holidays. In personal ritual observance as well, community is central. Prayer should be offered in a quorum of ten, Torah study is traditionally conducted with a partner. Life's major transition points, such as circumcision, bar-mitzvah, and marriage are, above all, milestones in one's deepening commitment to the community.

This emphasis on community in no way denies the validity of solitude; rather it seeks to engage the contemplative in an even higher pursuit, namely, that of bringing the entire community into an enlightened relationship with God. It is the purpose of all the *mitzvos*, the Divine commandments, to "draw down" God, who is utterly holy and removed, into the world (the Hebrew word for holiness – *kedushah* – means "separateness"), so that from within the world itself, a new revelation of the unity of the Creator should emerge.

So important is community that Kabbalistic writings consider *Knesset Yisroel*, the congregation of the People of Israel, as synonymous with the *Shechinah*, the Divine Presence on earth. For they share the same purpose, that of revealing God in the world, of being "a light unto the nations," in the words of the prophet (Isaiah 49:6). The *Shechinah* is the feminine element in creation, for it receives God's light, nurtures it, and reveals it in the world. Thus the union of God and the *Shechinah*, of the transcendent and the immanent, is not a static act. It is the constant bringing to birth of a new and ever-increasing awareness of God. Every single act, performed according to the laws of the Torah, brings about a greater revelation of God in the world, a greater unity between the Soul of the creation and the physical. Every act becomes a prayer, and as the Zohar says: "Prayer without intention is like a body without a soul."

This then, is the role of mankind – to lift back up to God, that which is furthest away. It is the reason why the soul leaves its pristine abode to dwell within the body, why God descends to create a world, and why the contemplative must eventually leave his retreat and unite with humanity. The contemplative is to the community what the soul is to the body. He gives it life, inspiration, and leads its members to a higher level. Then, if he finds that he must retreat again to his solitary path, it is because the final rectification has not yet been accomplished. He retreats, to draw from the source of inspiration, and returns again to water the garden of souls. This oscillation will continue until peace is finally made between body and soul, and God's presence so fills the earth that there is no place empty of Him.

"When will the Messiah come?" asks the Talmud. "When all the souls have come into the body." Then there will be no need for solitude, for the whole world will reveal His glory. The duality of God and the world will no longer exist, and the words of the prophet will be fulfilled: "On that day God will be One, and His Name One" (Zechariah 14:9).

The entire Torah and the entire world contain nothing but the light of the Infinite One (blessed be He) concealed within them. All the verses that speak of this, such as "There is no other than He" (Deuteronomy 4:35) and "I fill the heavens and the earth" (Jeremiah 23:24) are to be taken literally; for there is no act, word or thought in which the essence of Divinity is not constricted and hiding.

And so, when you look and see with your mind's eye, you will see the inner, life-force aspect of everything, not just its outer, superficial layer. You will see nothing but the divine power inside all things that is giving them life, being and existence at every moment.

And when you listen carefully to the inner voice within any physical sound that you hear, you will hear only the voice of God that, at that moment, is literally giving life and existence to the sound that you are hearing.

BAAL SHEM TOV
Kovetz Eliyahu §33

The Soul of Community

Every Jew has the power to bring the entire creation back to God, and to unite and uplift all the worlds. This is because a person is himself composed of all the worlds. His soul is from the upper world and his body from the lower one. When soul and body are bound together, he can unite all the worlds and bring them close to God. This is the aspect of peace. Peace exists between two opposites, such as the body and soul. When they are bound together in life, that is peace.

R. Nosson of Breslov
Likutey Halachos

I have heard that God wrote a book, which is the world, and He wrote a commentary to the book, which is the Torah; for the Torah explains how God can be found in the world.

Reb Simcha Bunim of Peshischa commented on the verse, "The whole earth is filled with Your acquisitions" (Psalms 104:24); that is, the whole world is filled with ways to acquire a knowledge of God and what He wants from us. For God created the entire world for this purpose – that from each thing we should learn how to serve Him, and to know that all is created for His glory.

R. Tzadok HaKohen of Lublin
Tzidkas HaTzaddik §216, Pri Tzaddik, Pesach 30

Among Breslover Chasidim

From a Visit to Berditchev in 1911

by Hillel Zeitlin

If a visitor to Berditchev wishes to hear a typical Jewish melody, let him listen to Reb Nissin Belzer's protege. If it is Berditchever Chasidic song he desires, he should go to the Karliner *shtiebel*.

When the holy Shabbos departs, and the Berditchever week arrives with its barrenness, darkness and destitution, the Karliner chasidim are still aflame. Their ecstasy has just begun, and they don't even dream of bidding farewell to the Shabbos Queen. I heard their singing from afar one *Motzoei Shabbos* and couldn't detect even a hint of sorrow. Now they are sitting in the palace of the Divine Presence – how can they bother themselves with hunger and pain, poverty and gloom? To be sure, each one of them has his own bundle of suffering at home. To be sure, these burdens are most difficult to bear. To be sure, many have aging daughters to marry off, bills and rent and tuition to pay, and an empty money-box to cover all expenses. If God so decrees, one must attempt to heal wife and children – and one is himself a bit sick. Old age encroaches, one's strength begins to fail, the world is stricken, there is no sustenance. Tear yourself apart – but what will you accomplish? One sits at the King's table, and when the Holy One is present, blessed be He, there is no room for worry. We Jews have a God who lives forever. The merit of Shabbos will stand by us. The old Karliner Rebbe is surely a good advocate Over There. Besides, why worry when we know that everything our Father does is for the good? "Even when I walk in the valley of the shadow of death, I shall fear no evil, for Thou art with me…"

However, if one would like to hear an altogether different sort of melody, if one would like to hear a melody born of the deepest and most difficult sorrow, if one would like to truly witness a Godly joy, if one would like to see ecstasy which is not the result of emotionalism or fervor but only of the most profound, lucid knowledge, if one would like to see how men can actually walk upon the earth and yet not be here, let him forbear to traverse the muddy Berditchever streets, let him cling to the crooked alleyways, let him pass by the ancient cemetery, the broad desolate field where the night-shadows fall on orphaned hills, and where one lonely, leafless tree at the edge of the meadow can bring one to tears. Afterwards, let him also pass the so-called "Lively *Shul*" – the *shul* nearest the old graveyard. Let him pass by many other such *shuls*, let him absorb the Jewish dejection and the special melancholy which can be felt in Jewish settlements. When the divinity of Shabbos is about to depart from her children, and dark reality peers out with her lackluster eyes, let him then betake himself to the *shtiebel* of the Breslover chasidim.

Let him bring along his own broken spirit. Let him prop himself up in a dark corner and hear sigh after sigh from the Breslover chasidim who sit around the table, listening to their Rebbe's teachings. Let him feel in their sighs an expression of the lecturer's phrase, "Such a yearning after God that it is unbearable." Let him listen well to what is being said. Let him not trouble himself that this or that interpretation of Scripture is not so smooth or tidy, or may be open to various objections. Let him hear the main point. Let him hear the tenor of the words, the greatest simplicity which emerges with the greatest wisdom, the most profound insights mentioned in passing without any indication that here, whole worlds have been laid bare, gradually touching upon everything that exists on earth and raising it up to the Heavens.

Let him feel here the cosmic pathos, which, after the moment of inner liberation, must be transformed to cosmic joy. Let him feel that here hovers the spirit of the great Rebbe, Reb Nachman of Breslov, who lifts men up from the darkest depths of hell to the highest everlasting light.

Let him later observe how silently, one by one, the chasidim leave the table, join hands, form a circle and begin to dance. In this dance not one awkward move can be detected, for every turn, every gesture, every inclination has been refined, ennobled, sanctified to the loftiest level.

You look, but you cannot believe your eyes. They seem to be ordinary people, simple Jews, not great scholars, perhaps not scholars at all. They look like common laborers and porters, yet such inwardness, depth of feeling, and clarity of insight, such spirituality in every gesture, every footstep, and every note of song is impossible to find elsewhere.

All the days of my childhood were spent among chasidim, and in my life I have had occasion to hear and to see various kinds of Chasidic singing and dancing, including some exceptional melodies from the old Chabad chasidim. But I never heard or saw anything equal to what I experienced in that poorly-lit, forlorn *shtiebel* of the Breslover chasidim in Berditchev. Their joy is a true joy, and their song is a song of redemption. They are free men. Say what you will, these people, particularly when among themselves, are no longer in exile. They are always at home – in Godliness. Outwardly, they may seem less impressive than other chasidim. But one who has an eye to glimpse what is going on within the next fellow must be astounded by the honest, wholesome rejoicing of these people, when through their dance, they talk to God.

As we approach the Breslover *shul*, my companion, whose sympathies do not lie with the chasidim, whispers, "Here we must walk more quietly." His observation is most appropriate. A certain quiet holiness rests upon this *shtiebel*. Quiet is the sigh, yet it splits the Heavens. Quiet is the discourse, yet it penetrates to the depths. Quiet is the dance, but through it you seem to be carried away, in spite of yourself, to other worlds. Quiet is the melody which suffuses your very being. Everything is quiet, everywhere.

Aside from the chasidim, a number of Jews come here from off the street. They come by chance or out of curiosity, not always innocent of a penchant for laughter or scorn – yet all remains quiet here. Everyone must listen. By his own choice or otherwise, the scoffer will be a scoffer no more. He must become sincere. This in itself testifies to the power of the spirit: that which is noble and strong must overcome that which is base and inferior.

During his exposition the speaker remarks, "The Jewish people must teach all the nations that there is a God in the world."

One of the scoffers comes over to me and murmurs, "He means that gentiles should attend his sermons...."

A little later, I see that very same scoffer watching everything with an expression of utter seriousness. He doesn't care to laugh anymore.

As the dance becomes especially beautiful and joyous, I observe a fourteen-year-old boy, one of the curious, tell his friend, "It would be so good if all Jews could be this happy with their faith!"

Indeed, it would be so good, my child, so good…

> Redemption depends on faith, whereas exile results from a lack of faith. The redemption will come when the Jewish people affirm their belief that everything that happens in the world and in the life of each individual, whether suffering or contentment, comes from God. Nothing is accidental. One must also believe that everything God does is for a person's good.
>
> If even a single group of friends could together reach this level of faith, the redemption would arrive immediately.
>
> R. Shimshon Barsky
> *Eitzos HaMevuoros*

❧ DISCIPLINE ☙

These are the laws that you shall set before them.

– Exodus 21:1

THERE ARE MANY DIFFERENT APPROACHES TO the practice of Torah. Some stress the ethical aspect of the commandments, others, the simple fulfillment of the *mitzvos* as God's will. Kabbalah sees them as spiritual practices – as acts done to achieve a realization of God. Reb Dovid Din used to call them "Jewish yoga," in the sense that, like yoga, they are a spiritual discipline that can bring about inner transformation.

Coming from a background in meditation, that approach always spoke to me the most. It cuts through all the questions of the historical truth of Torah, and stands it on a single criterion: Does it work?

I believe that it does. However, the answer to that question is deeply personal and requires years of practice and commitment.

A New Song

> Sing to the Lord a new song, His praise in the assembly of the pious.
>
> — *Psalms 149: part of the morning prayer service*

There are old men in my synagogue who have been reciting these words for over seventy years. I often wonder if they still mean them. I have been saying them for a much shorter time and must struggle daily with their repetitiveness. The same is true of ritual. The same is true of study. The same is true of meditation. So much of spiritual work seems to revolve around deeds that quickly become routine. Judaism, with its vast array of cyclical laws, is not unique in this. Ritual and repetition are at the heart of every religious tradition, so that even the most inspired seeker may soon find himself aground in the shallow waters of daily observance. It's known that the essence of spiritual work is to come to an ever-renewing vision of God. Although the heart and mind search for this, and the soul cries out for it, the tradition maintains its stoic insistence on the necessity of the discipline. Where, then, is the voice of the Living God?

Kabbalah perceives reality as multi-dimensional, composed of myriads of concentric spiritual worlds of ever-finer substance. Creation is like a rose-bud with each petal gently enfolded in the next. At the heart of them all is God, the most concealed, the most intimate. God's presence is the innermost point of creation, and it is He who enlivens and sustains all existence. Likewise, on the personal dimension, the consciousness of God is at the center of all human activity. Thus, at the heart of all loves is the love of God. The basis of all fear is the awe of His power. And the constant desire for the new and unique is, in actuality, a longing for the revelation of God, who recreates the entire world anew each second. Yet we can neither see, nor feel this presence, because creation is too "thick," and God is obscured. According to Jewish mystical thought, this is a direct result of the sin of Adam.

When classic rabbinic sources speak of Adam - the primary human image - they refer to a being so transcendent that the angels mistook him for God; whereas the fall of man is understood to mean a fall into the physical, from a body of light to "garments of skin" (Genesis 3:21). And when Adam - whose being embraced all of creation - fell, so did everything else. So too, in the realm of consciousness, Chasidic texts speak of fallen loves and fallen fears, in which a lesser, and often debased, emotion takes the place of that which arises from true communion with the Divine. Every relationship is a relationship with God, but when that core truth is hidden, the external world takes on an independent reality that deceives and entices the individual.

Thus, the goal of all spiritual work is to detach the seeker from the preoccupation with the outer trappings of reality and redirect the energies inward, to that place where infinity touches the soul; for the fallen attributes can never equal the power and ecstasy of the being in its source. Whereas fallen love is selfish, love of God is expansive. Fallen fears are obsessive; true fear is edifying. In Judaism, the return to the source is accomplished through the path of Torah, which lifts the fallen world back to God.

At first glance, the practice of Torah seems exceedingly difficult. There are 613 explicit commandments found in the Pentateuch, and together with the details of their observance, the number reaches the tens of thousands. Positive commandments require action of some kind, while negative ones demand a degree of restraint. There is barely an act in the day that does not come under the jurisdiction of the Law. Many of these acts are repetitious and a fair amount of them restrictive. Nonetheless, the purpose of all the *mitzvos* – the commandments – is to disengage the practitioner from the fallen aspects of reality and reinvest that energy in a vertical movement of the soul. For when the being no longer disperses itself horizontally, it begins to turn inward for fulfillment. "And God saw that the light was good," says the verse (Genesis 1:4). "Therefore he hid it away for the righteous," comments the Midrash. To which the Baal Shem Tov added, "Where did He hide it? In the Torah!"

One simple illustration of this process: Jewish law establishes a dress code for both men and women which puts great value on the trait of modesty. For instance, the sight of long-frocked chasidim is a common one in many American cities. This is meant less as a denial of the outside world than a cultivation of the inner one. It is a type of monastic gesture, albeit a worldly one, that understands that through modest dress and behavior, one comes to touch a depth of spirit within. The same holds true for most religions, and donning the "robes of initiation" signals a commitment to the pursuit of the inner life. The entire Torah can be understood in this way, the laws and rituals help define our relationship with God. Negative commandments preserve the purity of the soul, while positive ones direct its energies in spiritual channels. "Do not stray to another field, my daughter," they tell the soul, "Turn not away from here" (Ruth 2:8).

In the Jewish tradition, masters of the spirit are known as Tzaddikim – the Just. According to the Talmud, there are thirty-six hidden Tzaddikim in every generation, through whose merit the world is sustained. These individuals have touched the very core of truth within themselves, yet from without, they are completely unrecognizable. In this they reflect their Master, whose Presence is also hidden in the world. It is not through any intrinsic lack that the soul is hidden, rather, it is the very nature of spirit as something so personal, so interior and ultimately, so boundless, that it can never be fully expressed in this world. "I know that God is great," says the Psalm (Psalms 135:5). "I know," commented Rabbi Nachman of Breslov, "but I cannot tell another." The story is told about Rabbi Yosef Yitzchok Schneersohn, one of the great Chasidic Rebbes of the previous generation and an outstanding public figure, who was once asked by his chasidim, "Rebbe, we believe that you are a Tzaddik, yet how is that possible? Tzaddikim are supposed to be hidden, and we see you." "How do you know you see all of me?" he replied.

The purpose of the *mitzvos* is to engender a union with God. The very word "*mitzvah*" relates to the grammatical root of the word "to join." Furthermore, Judaism does not consider the *mitzvos* as merely expedient means for reaching the goal of enlightenment; they are themselves considered the ultimate expression of God's will, and Kabbalah speaks of their mystical nature as conduits for divine influx. The practice of *mitzvos* refines the being and opens it to movements of the spirit. Commitment to their observance, despite repetition and boredom, is what ultimately reveals the inner light. Slowly, a window is opened to the soul, which begins to shine in all the corners of one's life.

This same process is reflected in every discipline, be it art, religion or craft. No great artist ever mastered his field without first being mastered by it. And nothing new was ever created that did not build upon the achievements of the past. Only commitment to the exterior form of the craft, despite the tediousness of the process, allows the inner source of creativity to reveal itself. Ultimately, a person touches the core of life, which then flows out and fills the previous static forms with new meaning. When, through the ritual, one reaches the point of infinity in the soul, the ritual itself becomes the setting for the revelation of infinite content. "A person who studies Torah selflessly becomes like an ever-renewing spring," says the Talmud. Likewise, in the mystical consciousness, every detail of creation has the potential for infinite meaning, because the presence of the Infinite God lies beneath the surface waiting to be revealed.

So it is on the spiritual path. Inner rejuvenation only comes when the outer vessel has been set in place. Then the very forms that originally seemed restrictive become liberating, for the practitioner has been freed from the fallen nature of reality. The rose of the tradition unfolds to reveal the presence of the Holy One within, and the flow of life newly released finds no better vehicle of expression than the very words of prayer one has been saying all along.

Thus, in Judaism, this world is never abandoned. It provides the tools with which we search for God, and ultimately becomes the channel through which God reveals Himself in our lives. If our words of prayer have become routine, it is because we have not been saying them long enough. One must persevere with the practice despite the difficulty, until the forms reveal their inner meaning. To keep digging for treasure long after one has abandoned hope of ever finding it. God gives us the tools, and we must work with them. In doing this, we build the vessels to receive. Ultimately, God, in His love and compassion, fills them with His presence. "The hidden things are the Lord our God's, but the revealed things are ours and our children's forever, that we may do all the words of this Torah" (Deuteronomy 29:28).

> "Sing to the Lord a new song; sing to the Lord all the earth" (Psalms 96:1)
>
> Even idolaters recognize God as the Creator and First Cause of reality. What they fail to understand is the essential difference between God and a human creator. For the works of the latter continue to exist even after their maker has left them, such as a watch, which continues to run, once it has been assembled.
>
> God, however, directs the creation constantly, with His infinite power, and were He to remove His influence for even a moment, everything would revert to nothingness.
>
> Therefore, idolaters sing an old song, because to them, God is only the First Cause. But Israel sings to Him a new song, because in His goodness, He renews each day the work of creation.
>
> R. Meir Leibush Malbim
> *Commentary on Sefer Tehilim*

Heart of Stone

A parable of the Baal Shem Tov

Once there was a king who had a wise and clever son. In order to develop his son's gifts fully, the king sent him off to a distant land where he could study with the leading scholars in the world. The prince spent several years there immersed in his studies, and amassed a great deal of knowledge. Finally, he returned home to the king, who welcomed him with great joy. Nevertheless, the king had to put his son to a test, to see if what he had learned was of true value.

In the palace courtyard lay a large stone, too big for any single person to budge. The king called his son outside. "Do you see this stone?" he asked. "Here is your test. Lift up this stone and carry it to the top of that tower." The prince thought and thought, but could not formulate any way to move that heavy load. The more time went by, the more depressed he became, for he could not fulfill his father's wish. The king, for his part, waited patiently, giving his son ample time to apply all the knowledge that he learned.

When the king saw that there was no hope, and that all the wisdom his son had acquired could not help him, he called the boy aside. "Do you think I would ask you such an impossible task as to carry this stone to the palace's highest tower?" he asked. "That is not my intention at all. Rather, I want you to take a hammer and break the stone into little pieces. Then you can lift it up a piece at a time."

The stone is the human heart; the hammer is our words of prayer. If we apply hammer to stone, slowly, after years of effort, the heart is broken and can be uplifted to God.

> These words, which I command you today, shall be upon your heart. (Deuteronomy 6:6)
> Why does the verse command us to set the words of Torah upon our hearts? Surely they should be in our hearts?
> The answer is that it is not always simple to put the words of Torah in our hearts. But at least if they are on our hearts, when our hearts opens up, they will fall in.
>
> R. MENACHEM MENDEL OF KOTSK
> *Emes v'Emunah*

The Power of Prayer

There was once a simple Israeli worker from Jerusalem, who, though he had been married for many years, had never received the blessing of children. He had been to all the specialists, but to no avail. "Hair will grow on the palm of your hand before you see a child," they had bluntly told him. After years of hope and despair, he finally heard of the great miracles wrought by the prayers of Rabbi Yisrael Abuchatzira, the great Baba Sali, of blessed memory.

With an expectant heart, he traveled two hours to Netivot, to the synagogue of the Baba Sali. When he arrived, he found a long line of petitioners already ahead of him, and had to wait hours before entering to receive a blessing. Finally, his turn arrived. He entered the Tzaddik's room, nervous, eyes downcast, clutching a small piece of paper on which he had written his only request: Children! He sat down and placed the paper on the table before the Baba Sali. The Tzaddik opened it, then put it down. "*Matzav avud,*" he said, "a lost case." Before he fully understood what happened, the man was whisked out of the chamber by the attendants to make room for the next petitioner. Shocked, brokenhearted, he returned to his home.

The next day, however, when the people began assembling

DISCIPLINE

for blessings, there he was in line again. Again he waited several hours. Again he entered the room, put his request upon the table, and again, he heard the same answer, "a lost case." Yet, when the next day arrived, there he was again, and the next day again! Every single day, as long as the Baba Sali was receiving people for blessings, the man would be there in line, at times waiting hours. And always he would receive the same sad answer, "a lost case."

Finally, after almost a year, the family of the Baba Sali took pity on this man and approached the great saint with their request. "Rabbeinu Yisrael," they said, "this poor man has been coming to you for a year straight now, and every time you give him the same answer. Can't you tell him to stop coming already? It's too heartbreaking to continue."

"How long has it been?" Rabbi Abuchatzira inquired.

"We've counted, and today is his two hundredth visit!"

The Baba Sali agreed to talk with him.

That afternoon, the man entered as usual, and placed his slip of paper on the table before the Baba Sali. This time the Tzaddik did not even pick it up.

"Listen, my friend," he said kindly, "you have been coming to me every day for a very long time. Haven't I already told you that it is a lost case? Go home, why do you insist on coming to me?"

The man lifted his eyes. "I come to you every day, and I will keep coming to you every day because I believe in prayer, and I believe God listens to your prayers, and that you are the only one in the world who can help me."

"Do you really believe that?" the Baba Sali responded, rising from his chair. "If so, go out right now and buy a baby carriage!"

The man gave a start and then ran out of the room. "I got a blessing!" he cried in joy. That night he presented his wife with a beautiful, new baby carriage.

Nine months later, he had a son.

❧

> A Jew must never abandon hope, not in matters of the body nor of the soul. Even if he has sunk to the lowest level and sinned in ways that *teshuvah* itself will not remedy, he must never abandon hope and think that he can no longer extricate himself from his predicament; for there is simply no such a thing as despair for a Jew. God is always able to help.
>
> Indeed, the entire foundation of the Jewish nation came only after the utter despair of Abraham and Sarah, as it is written: "Who would have told Abraham that Sarah would nurse a child? (Genesis 21:7), for it never even occurred to them. Even when the angels promised them this, Sarah, who was a righteous woman and believed that God was all-powerful, nevertheless laughed inside herself, the idea being so incredible, and Abraham being so old.
>
> But really, this was arranged by God in order that the very formation of the Jewish nation come precisely after such resignation. Thus, it is the very essence of a Jew to believe that there is no despair at all, and that God is always able to help.
>
> R. TZADOK HAKOHEN OF LUBLIN
> *Divrei Sofrim 16*

CONSCIOUSNESS

You should know this day, and take to your heart, that the Lord is God: in heaven above and upon the earth below, there is nothing else.

– Deuteronomy 4:39

BECAUSE OF MY BACKGROUND IN BUDDHISM, I have always been drawn to Torah teachings that deal with states of consciousness and shifts in human perception. Thus, I have long studied the works of one of the greatest Jewish mystics – at least the one who spoke the most openly about mystical experience – Rabbi Nachman of Breslov. Another great Chasidic teacher, Rabbi Tzadok HaKohen of Lublin, also had profound things to say about clarity of consciousness, and the power of Torah study to remove the veil of the imagination that obscures our vision of absolute truth. Both these great Masters are a constant source of inspiration for me.

At the Center

> Rabbi Yosef, the son of Rabbi Yehoshua ben Levi, fainted and died, but was revived.
> "What did you see?" his father asked him.
> "I saw an upside-down world. The high ones were low and the low ones were high."
> "My son, you saw a clear world. And as for us Torah scholars, how were we?"
> "Just as we are here, so we are there," he said.
> – Babylonian Talmud: BAVA BASRA 10b

In the second chapter of *Mishnah Torah*, Maimonides' classic compendium of Jewish law and belief, the author begins a discussion of "matters exceedingly deep, beyond the grasp of the average person... matters that the mouth cannot utter, the ear cannot hear, nor the heart clearly understand." Having previously discussed God's Oneness and Transcendence, the great sage now turns to a discussion of God's way of knowing, and the vast difference between that and our own: "The Holy One does not know with a knowledge outside of Himself, as do we, for we and our knowledge are not one. Rather, the Creator, His Knowledge and His Life are One... Therefore, He does not know creatures as we know them, rather, He knows them because of Himself. He knows Himself, and therefore knows all...."

It has always seemed to me that these words are significant more for what they say about us than what they say about God, for they suggest an alternative way of knowing – as though this present moment holds within it two perspectives, from above and from below, and that it is possible to change the direction of our thought. For if human existence is somehow swept up in God's act of self-knowledge, then the true nature of our consciousness is very different than the way we presently experience it. Maimonides' words contain a subtle challenge – to overturn our perception and know ourselves not as we do now, but as beings known by God.

In the writings of later commentators, this idea from *Mishnah Torah* is expanded upon: "We and our knowledge are not one." That is, there is an essential difference between what we are and what we know. Knowledge is not intrinsic to us, but received from without. It is gathered one detail at a time, each point we learn adding information that was not there before, until a complete picture is formed. However, the opposite must be said of God. Since there is nothing outside of Him, knowledge cannot add anything to His essence. His knowledge of creation is therefore not acquired, but part of His knowledge of Himself. In Maimonides' words: "He is the knower, the known and the act of knowing."

But there is a deeper allusion in these words. To say that our knowledge of reality is collected over time means that it is the individual's consciousness that is constantly assembling reality into an intelligible whole. The world becomes meaningful to me as I construct it within, and precisely because of my perception, life is invested with value and importance. To put it more simply, in the very act of knowing, I create the universe – with myself at its center.

This generates a cognitive problem, and also a moral one. It means that wherever we look, we see only ourselves; that we are boxed in by our own mode of perception. For in judging the world, we naturally favor those things that strengthen our ego, and reject those things that challenge it. In the *Guide for the Perplexed*, Maimonides writes that before the Fall, Adam and Eve perceived creation in the objective terms of truth and falsehood. After the sin, they perceived it in terms of good and bad, as though the fall of man can be understood as a descent into subjectivity.

This is not only how we relate to the world, even spiritual growth can become defined in terms of personal goals. The constant desire for "higher" realization can also be an expression of the ego. What has been termed "spiritual materialism" is really a result of the self assigning meaning to reality – even to God! We live in an upside-down world, in which even the Creator becomes subsidiary to our will and desires. To switch perspectives and see the world from the true viewpoint is the real goal of spiritual work. If not, then all of our knowledge, including that of the spirit, will be interpreted through the criteria of the self.

Practically speaking, the importance of religious traditions lies in their ability to diminish our self-attachment and establish the proper relationship between God and the world. It is said of the revelation at Sinai that God had to force the Israelites to accept the Torah; its demands were so much beyond their ability to comprehend. It forced them into a new mode of thinking; it forced them into a new order of relationship. Yet, by placing God at the center of reality, the Torah breathes life into creation. It presents the seeker with a body of laws and ethics that can radically transform his world view.

Ultimately, spiritual growth is not about the self at all. The real work begins when we step out of the center and define ourselves within a larger framework of meaning. As Rabbi Israel of Salant, one of the great ethical teachers of the last century said, "Caring for the other fellow's physical needs fulfills my spiritual ones." Life then becomes defined in terms of others: family, community, humanity and ultimately, the Oneness and Presence of the Divine.

But in order to reach this final stage – the transcendence of the self as final mediator of truth – one must be ready to die for it. If spiritual practice does not tear down one's conception of the world, if it does not uproot the foundations of one's perception and rebuild them from the top down, if it does not change in the most fundamental way the nature of how a person thinks, then one is quite literally doing it backwards. "The Torah only lives in one who kills himself over it," says the Talmud. For the Torah's goal is to stand reality on its head, to destroy the world and rebuild it in the Divine image. "Behold, I have put My words in your mouth… to root out and to pull down, to destroy and to overthrow – in order to build and to plant" (Jeremiah 1:10).

Only in the moment when everything that we know is overturned can we see the world from a true perspective, in a context of Oneness and as a manifestation of the Divine. In the moment when self-preoccupation ceases, we become vessels for something much greater. "As clay in the potter's hand, so are you in My hand, O house of Israel" (ibid. 18:6). From this higher vantage point, life's purpose is to invest all creation with God's Glory, and to promote unity among all its components. This knowledge is not separate from God, but Divinity itself: it is the very life of creation.

And so, Rabbi Yosef, the son of Rabbi Yehoshua ben Levi, saw an upside-down world – a clear world – from a perspective very different than our own. But only when he died to the fiction of this present reality as the center of existence. Only when we can die to this world, as did Rabbi Yosef, can we behold a true picture of reality. Then, one is freed from the self as dictator of meaning, to become a vessel for the Holy One – knowing ourselves as we are known from Above. As the verse says, "Every one that is called by My Name; I have created him for My Glory; I have formed him, yea I have made him" (Isaiah 43:7).

Wherever a person directs his thoughts, that is where he is. If he thinks negative thoughts, he is attached to negativity. If he trusts in God's loving-kindness, then his soul is attached there, and "loving-kindness will surround him" (Psalms 32:10). Thus, he should constantly immerse himself in God.

In fact, one need not even place his thoughts on Divinity; but simply imagine that he is already completely absorbed in the Divine light.

Baal Shem Tov
Baal Shem Tov al HaTorah, Amud HaTefilah §31, Ekev §31

Empty fantasies prevent the knowledge and awareness of God from entering the heart. I have heard that the land of Egypt represents the power of the imagination. Thus, the First Commandment states, "I am the Lord your God, who took you out of the land of Egypt" – that is, from empty fantasies – and raised your consciousness to cling to Me.

This is the whole purpose of the *mitzvos*, which are said to be "a remembrance of the exodus from Egypt." They redeem us from illusion, from Egypt, which is the very opposite of Torah and *mitzvos*.

A person's main battle against his evil inclination lies in overcoming the fantasies and illusions of his heart and mind.

R. Tzadok HaKohen of Lublin
Tzidkas HaTzaddik §205, 207, 208

Neighbors

A parable of the Baal Shem Tov

In a certain city, in adjoining homes, lived two men. One was a brilliant Torah scholar, whose life was dedicated to learning, and who never left the study-hall. The other was a simple worker, who lived "by the sweat of his brow."

The Torah scholar would rise before dawn, study and meditate several hours before prayer, then pray with tremendous concentration. He would continue his studies the entire day, breaking only to eat. Finally, he would return home late at night, happy with all the Torah that he had learned and the prayers he had recited.

The simple worker would also rise early, but he would run to *shul* and speed through the prayers with almost no concentration. Then he would rush off to his difficult job, only to return home in the evening, broken and exhausted. He would grab a bite to eat, then run off to the study hall. Being too tired to open a book or listen to a lecture, he made do with a quick evening prayer, then returned home to collapse on his bed. His soul was troubled over his difficult life.

Every morning these two men would meet, since the doors of their homes were adjacent. Whenever the poor man would see his scholarly neighbor, and realize how filled with

Torah his life was, he would let out a deep sigh. And when the scholar would see the poor worker, whose life was empty of Torah and prayer, he would give him a disparaging look, as if to say, "See how different you and I are…"

Years went by. The two men eventually passed away and appeared before the Heavenly Court. The scholar came with all of his learning in hand; the worker came with nothing.

"Look at all this Torah study and the magnificent prayers of this rabbi!" the scholar's defending angel said, as he piled up mounds and mounds of *chidushei Torah* and shining prayers.

"But he was arrogant in his learning, and belittled his poor neighbor," the accusing angel said.

The poor man was brought forth next. He stood trembling before the Heavenly Tribunal.

"What do you have to show for yourself?" they asked.

"Nothing," he sighed. "All my life I slaved for a living, and I had no time for Torah study."

The court brought forth the scales. On one side, they piled up all the scholar's study and prayers, and on the other side, his disdain for his poor neighbor. The disdain outweighed them all.

Next, onto the scale they put the poor man's entire life, devoid of Torah and prayer, and on the other side, his heartbreaking sigh at seeing his scholarly neighbor.

The sigh pushed the scales all the way down.

Neighbors

A Jew toils the whole day in the marketplace, until he almost forgets that there is a Creator. When the time for the afternoon prayer arrives, he suddenly remembers that he has to pray, and lets out a heartfelt sigh, thinking how he wasted his whole day in mundane affairs. He runs to some side-street and prays, though he doesn't even understand what he is saying. Nonetheless, his prayers are very special and precious to God, and his sigh splits open the heavens.

BAAL SHEM TOV
Magen Avraham, parshas Balak

Each person must ask: "When will my deeds reach those of my Forefathers, Abraham, Isaac and Jacob?" (*Tanna d'Vei Eliyahu*, 25).

Though it is impossible to attain this level without God's help, one *can* deeply long for it. Indeed, this is the whole person – to yearn for God with all of one's heart and soul. And according to the intensity of one's longing, so is God's longing for him, as it says: "As your heart is to your beloved, so is your beloved's heart to you" (*Sifri* on Deuteronomy 27), and "God is your shadow" (Psalms 121:5); that is, He mirrors us like a shadow. Through this, each person can fulfill this longing, according to his level. God will help him achieve his true purpose in life, which is to be His "planting of beauty" (Isaiah 60:31), the seed of Abraham, Isaac and Jacob.

R. TZADOK HAKOHEN OF LUBLIN
Machshavos Chorutz 3

THE SOUL

When I call, answer me, my righteous God;
amidst distress, You have broadened me.

– Psalms 4:1

ONE OF THE MOST DIFFICULT PERIODS IN MY life occurred in my late twenties. I was renting a small room in Jerusalem, my health was poor, and I was lonely and alone. Back in the States, Reb Dovid Din had recently passed away, and in Israel, all my friends had already married. (I remained single until I was thirty-seven.)

I recall lying in bed one day under tremendous emotional stress – so much so that I felt I could not even move. I lay there, burnt out and broken inside. Yet – amazingly – at that very moment, I also felt some pure spark of absolute joy welling up inside me. I couldn't understand where it came from. It was as if the pain had actually cleared something away to let it become revealed.

I never reached that level of emotional pain again, nor have I felt that spark of joy again.

Through a Dark Passage

The path of the soul is not simple, for it travels a tortuous route in this world. Twisting and turning in the course of life, moving from unity to dissolution before reaching the final destination of wholeness. But in the process, it gains a depth and fullness that it never would have attained had it not initially set out.

The soul begins in unity. Prior to entering this world, it exists in a state of attachment to the Divine. It gazes in a light that shines across creation and learns a supernal wisdom. However, at the moment of birth, this original connection is lost. As the soul descends into the world, it becomes fragmented and broken, splintered into millions of pieces and scattered across creation. Falling like rain upon the fields, it seeps deeply into all things, animate and inanimate. It is these drops of soul, embedded within the objects of this world, which give life and vitality to existence.

Thus, while the soul is focused in the body, its influence does not end there. Chasidic texts explain that elements of a person's soul can be found in all of his belongings – the very reason that makes these items uniquely his. Soul extends even further, beyond one's immediate realm, to touch those things that are not yet in one's possession. Thus, the crops of the field, the fish in the sea, all grow and develop due to the far-flung sparks of human soul within them. And because their life-source is derived from a particular individual, these things will, over time, re-enter his domain. It is at that moment they can be uplifted, for the path of spiritual growth lies in collecting these soul-fragments and reintegrating them into the being.

This means to say that all of life is a gathering up of soul. In every encounter with the physical world, in the food we eat, the clothing we wear, lost fragments of soul are being regained. All of them must be collected, for if even a fraction of the soul were to be missing, a person would have to travel across the world to retrieve it. However, physical objects do not yield up their soul so easily. More often than not, material attachments tend to pull a person down, concealing any level of spirituality that has been attained. Soul is elicited from the things of this world by using them in a *sacred* way. Judaism regards the human being's role as that of a fulcrum for creation, with the power to uplift reality and invest the world with holiness. At the heart of Jewish spirituality is the practice of *mitzvos*, the commandments, whose primary concern is the sanctification of the physical world. Every *mitzvah*, explains the Kabbalah, releases another aspect of soul from its imprisonment in the physical.

From another perspective, we can say that the pursuit of soul manifests itself in the consciousness as the search for *meaning* in life – that essential quality that lies beneath the surface of the world. Like soul, the search for meaning can propel an individual to the most distant places on earth. Seen in these terms, the Torah presents itself as an all-encompassing system that seeks to align reality within a vast meaning-framework. The Torah is the "blueprint" of creation, in the words of the Midrash. There is nothing so mundane that it stands beyond the realm of its concern. In this, the Torah invests all life with the ultimate meaning that is born out of the relationship with God.

Sparks of soul are not just scattered throughout the physical world; they are embedded in the consciousness as well. Within the daily flood of ideas and emotions, fragments of soul – thoughts of holiness and longing for God – can be found. These too must be sought out and gathered up. True spiritual work always addresses the whole person, the inner dimension as well as the outer. In Jewish spirituality, the path of *mitzvos* is accompanied by that of prayer and Torah study – the service of the heart and of the mind. These bring all facets of the being into relationship with the Divine, and all of life into the structure of meaning.

The search for soul can lead a person across the world, and into the innermost recesses of the being. There are times when the presence of soul shines forth brightly, and other times when it remains completely hidden. Kabbalah teaches that in the soul's initial descent to this world, the highest sparks invariably fall to the lowest levels – the dark side of human nature. This means that the encounter with evil is a crucial element in the process of reintegration. Only by entering the dark places of the being – moments of anger, depression, or despair – can one redeem the sparks of soul that are trapped there. Without a willingness to confront this negative side of the personality, the individual will forever remain incomplete.

Thus, Judaism understands the most important spiritual work to occur precisely in times of darkness, in the depths of personal exile. "From the bowels of hell I cried out, and You heard my voice" (Jonah 2:3). Only by maintaining faith and hope in the moment of crisis can the fallen fragments of soul be redeemed, so that out of the greatest dissolution, the greatest wholeness can be formed; for soul is born out of its very opposite. Likewise, the need to find meaning in the face of mortal suffering is one of the most intrinsic aspects of being human. As anyone who has encountered personal tragedy knows, it is precisely through the struggle with hopelessness and despair that the greatest levels of integration and spiritual awareness can emerge.

The passage of the soul, from original unity, through darkness and dissolution, to final integration, is paralleled in the cosmos by the universal redemptive process. Kabbalah teaches that at the birth of creation, sparks of Divine Presence – the soul of the world – were scattered throughout existence. By means of exile and redemption these sparks are collected. "Know that your descendants shall be foreigners in a land that is not their own," God told Abraham. "They shall be afflicted… and afterwards, they shall come out with great wealth" (Genesis 15:14). For when all these pieces have been gathered, the soul of the world will be complete, and the presence of God will be revealed in creation.

Thus, the history of the world is the history of soul, the history of humanity's search for meaning. Just as an individual must confront suffering in order to redeem the most precious elements of his being, so must all of humanity. In doing so, it can emerge "with great wealth." Mystical sources explain that in the future age of redemption, it will be revealed that the darkest moments of history were actually the times that held the greatest light – a truth that is impossible for us now to comprehend. "Behold, there is a place by Me," said God to Moses. "I will put you in a cleft of the rock, and will cover you with My hand while I pass by: and I will remove My hand and you shall see My back, but

Through a Dark Passage

My face shall not be seen" (Exodus 33:22-23). Only looking back will we see how God was present in the places He had previously been concealed, and how soul was made manifest in the face of the greatest despair.

☙

> When a person wants to make a small container larger, he must first break it.
>
> So too, when God wants to bestow goodness upon a person whose "container" is too small, He visits upon him some manner of sickness or pain. Thus, He breaks his small container in order to make it big enough to hold more blessings.
>
> God's intentions are only for the best.
>
> REB LEVI YITZCHOK OF BERDITCHEV
> *Kedushas Levi, Vayechi*

The Paper Piano

When the Nazis took control of Germany in 1933, they did not discriminate. When the box-cars rolled into the death camps, there was no favoritism. Young and old, men and women, the healthy and infirm, all were destined for the same end. In fact, if a person had talents, it was best to keep them a secret, because if the Nazis found out, precisely there the torture would begin. They would mangle an artist's hands, cripple an athlete's legs. Nothing was sacred in Nazi Germany.

A very special man lived in Berlin before the war. Naftali Horowitz was his name. Naftali was an extraordinarily gifted musician. A child prodigy on the piano, he had toured Europe before his tenth birthday. In his mature years, his annual concerts were the talk of the town. Music was his life and his joy. It was the breath of his lungs, the beat of his heart.

But when Hitler came into power, all that changed. At first, Naftali was forbidden to give public recitals. Then, he was no longer permitted to teach his young German pupils. His options became so limited that, in the end, only a few faithful Jewish youths continued their studies with him. But on his own, Naftali practiced constantly, and in that, he found solace.

The Paper Piano

However, even that blessing was soon to end, for when the deportations began, Naftali was separated from his home, his family, his music, from everything he ever knew and loved. He was deported, together with so many others, as part of the Final Solution. Naftali ended up in the concentration camp at Dachau, in Western Germany.

Unlike Auschwitz or Treblinka, Dachau was a labor camp. Here the prisoners were worked to death, instead of being killed upon arrival. There is no way to describe the agony, the pain, and the despair that racked these poor men's lives. Every day brought new tortures, greater cruelty, and an ever-enveloping darkness.

Each morning, in burning heat or freezing cold, several thousand prisoners would stand in the camp courtyard for roll call. Afterwards, they would march into the woods, into the stone quarries, into the swamps, to saw, hew, dig – to be beaten, tortured and shot. And every night, the survivors would return to their barracks, broken and despairing.

But Naftali was different; he was extraordinarily gifted. He had been at Dachau for only a short time, little more than a week, when he realized that there was only one way he could survive – by means of his music. He decided that he must keep practicing. But what could he do? He made covert inquiries through the underground channels and learned that there was no piano at Dachau: no music was ever to be heard in this God-forsaken place. And even assuming that a piano had been found, it would have been unlikely for the Germans to let him play. But Naftali had to have his music; he had to practice his art.

So a solution was found. Over a period of a week, through bribery and barter, Naftali managed to have smuggled out of the camp office a roll of heavy, white paper – about a meter long, and a foot wide. In addition, he managed to get hold of a small bottle of black ink. One night, when his bunk-mates had all fallen asleep, he sat down, plucked some threads from his tattered shirt-sleeve, and made a small wad-like brush. With this, he carefully drew the keys of a piano on the sheet of paper. Afterwards, he rolled up the paper in an old piece of cloth, tied it with a string and hid it under his bed. Every night after labor, he would remove the paper piano, roll it out and play. This simple paper piano was for him a source of life and strength. Once again, throughout the day, music would flow in his mind. Each night he would practice a different piece: a Beethoven concerto, a Mozart sonata, a Chopin Nocturne. He would return to his bunk, depleted, broken – but as soon as his fingers touched the paper keys, a new life would enter into him. In the dim cell, the other prisoners – pale, lifeless shadows – would prop themselves up upon their beds, lean on bruised elbows and watch Naftali play. In the dark, moonlit room he would give his virtuoso performances to these lost souls. In his graceful gestures, each man would hear a different melody; a Polish waltz, a Gypsy tune, a Chasidic *niggun*. Thus it continued for several months. For Naftali Horowitz, life began at night. When the screaming devils of the day were silent, a divine music would play in his heart.

It happened one night, as Naftali was practicing, that a newcomer to the bunk interrupted his performance.

"Hey, Mister," the man whispered. Naftali looked up. "Do you know that in Terezin, the camp where I just came from, they're putting together an orchestra?"

"What's it to me?" Naftali retorted.

"You should audition. If they accept you, they will treat you good. Who knows, maybe you will survive the war."

The Paper Piano

Naftali thought about the possibility of an audition as he lay on his bunk before sleep. Audition...before whom?... on what? There was no piano here at Dachau, and they certainly were not going to send him elsewhere to perform. Besides, the camp Commandant was a cruel and unyielding man. Naftali turned over the idea in his mind several times before sleep overcame him. No, it was impossible, and he dismissed it. By the shrill wake-up siren of the next morning, the thought was already forgotten.

Several weeks passed and life did not change. Inmates came and went, lived and died. Naftali's life depended upon his paper piano.

Then, one day, a hideous rumor began to circulate through the camp, until finally, it was confirmed. In two weeks' time, the entire camp, thousands of men, were being shipped out – sent to Auschwitz to die.

The complete and utter hopelessness that hung over the camp that week was unspeakable. Dozens of men simply gave up their lives before the German guards' rifles, rather than face the coming deportation. Even Naftali found no solace in his music, and he could scarcely bring himself to practice. Then, one night as he lay on his bunk, the words of that inmate (now dead) came back to him: Terezin – an orchestra – an audition – maybe he would live. But how? How could he do it? On what could he audition? Before whom could he play? He thought hard, and prayed for strength. There was one chance. One slim hope. He had to take it.

The next morning after roll call, as the prisoners separated into their respective work units, Naftali cautiously edged up to a German soldier whom he recognized as working in the Commandant's office.

"Herr Mueller," he whispered quickly, "Let me have just a word with you. I am a concert musician. I toured Europe many times before the war. They are assembling an orchestra in Terezin. I can play in it - if the Commandant will let me audition. If they accept me, it will be a feather in his cap - and yours. Speak to him."

"Jew, what do you want from me," the officer replied tersely. "Leave me alone, go to your work."

Naftali removed a package of cigarettes from under his shirt - black-market stock. He slipped it to the officer, who quickly put it in his pocket.

"I'll see what I can do," he muttered.

That evening, as the prisoners returned from their work, the officer motioned discreetly to Naftali. He went over to him.

"The Commandant said that tomorrow morning, immediately after roll call, you are to go to his office for an audition. And he says that you must bring your own instrument."

Morning came. Naftali stood nervously through the roll call. Immediately afterwards, as the men disassembled in the courtyard, he turned and walked cautiously towards the Commandant's office. A German guard at the door was apparently expecting his arrival and accompanied him in. There sat the Commandant and several of his top officers waiting for the show. As Naftali walked through the door, the guard behind him gave him a kick that sent him flying into the room. The officers roared with laughter as he fell onto the floor. Naftali got up, dusted himself off and stood at the front of the room. The Commandant spoke first.

"Well, Jew, we hear that you are a musician, and that you want to perform for us. Tell us, what is your instrument?"

The Paper Piano

His eyes fell upon the small bag Naftali held in his hand – it could have been a flute or a clarinet.

"I am a concert pianist," Naftali replied. The room once again broke into raucous laughter.

"Oh, really?" chuckled the Commandant. "And why do we never hear you practicing? Are you hiding a grand piano in your bunk, or perhaps a spinet? Maybe it is in your little bag, there?"

Naftali waited quietly for the Commandant to finish speaking. Then he drew the cord of the bag, removed the paper piano and spread it out on the table. The officers howled again with laughter. One of them, however, lost his temper. He removed his gun from his holster and pointed it straight at Naftali.

"Are you making fun of us, Jew? I'm going to kill you right now."

"Sit down, Hans. Sit down, Hans," his friends all called to him. "Let the Jew have his audition."

The Commandant chuckled and said, "Well, Jew, what will you play for us today?"

Naftali answered, "I am going to play Franz Liszt's Sonata in B minor. Opus number 168." The officers roared again with laughter. "Play it loud, Jew. Play it loud," they all called, "It will be your last performance."

Naftali sat down. He laid his hands for a moment across the paper keyboard. He took a deep breath, and then he started playing. Slowly his fingers moved across the keys, gently they touched each note. His body swayed to an internal rhythm. His left foot kept a steady beat. The music picked up speed. His fingers moved faster. Waves of emotion poured through his hands. They raced back and forth across the keyboard. They swept across the painted notes with beauty and vigor, pausing, skipping, dancing. In his mind he heard every note, every nuance. Sweat ran down his face. Never had he played with such intensity, such feeling. Not a sound was heard, but the room became filled with a silent music.

The Nazis sat silently. They did not interrupt. They did not take their eyes off him. For twenty minutes he played, and they sat transfixed. Finally, Naftali reached the end of the piece. His hands slowed down. His fingers gently stroked the closing notes. They lingered on the final chords. Then he stopped, sighed, and rested his hands on the table before him. The room was silent. Slowly, one by one, the officers rose from their chairs and left the room. Their eyes were upon the floor; they did not look in his direction.

At last, only the Commandant remained. He sat for a long time engrossed in thought. Then he rose. His eyes met Naftali's. They held there for a long moment, and then the Commandant looked away. He turned from the room and entered his office, leaving Naftali alone. Five minutes later the door opened. The Commandant walked over to Naftali. In his hand was a piece of official stationary with his signature. He handed it to Naftali. "Take this." he said, "Tomorrow you are going to Terezin."

Naftali Horowitz was transferred to Terezin concentration camp, where he played in the camp orchestra. He survived the war.

The Penny Candle

Heard from Rabbi Shlomo Carlebach

I will tell you a story, although you won't believe it. I wouldn't have believed it either, had I not seen it with my own eyes. But it happened; I was there.

The year was 1942, Poland, in the camps. I was in Auschwitz. We were so many poor souls clinging together, hungry, afraid. We could barely find enough support for ourselves, much less anyone else. But there was one man in our bunk different from all the rest. He was a Tzaddik. More than that, until today I believe he was one of the thirty-six. You know, the thirty-six hidden Tzaddikim on whom the whole world stands. His name was Reb Aharon. For the entire time I knew him, I never once heard him complain. It was the deepest hell, yet he never uttered a bad word. In fact, he managed to give help to others. There was a small group of us who clung to him, followed him around. What could we do, he was the only warmth and light we had.

Winter came, and it was bitterly cold. Such hopelessness hung in the air. Then came the announcement. Several days before Chanukah, the Germans declared that anybody found lighting candles would be shot. Well, for us, we could not dream of facing that threat. But what about Reb Aharon?

We whispered among ourselves. Could it be that Chanukah would pass and Reb Aharon would fail to bless the lights? No, impossible. But where would he get the candles?

The first night of Chanukah arrived. Our little group kept our eyes on him. We weren't going to let him out of our sight. All night you had to stay in the bunker. If they caught you outside, they would shoot you. 9:00 P.M., 10:00 P.M., 11:00. I started to doze off. When I caught myself, I realized that Reb Aharon had slipped out. I roused the others and we stole out after him. We followed his tracks in the snow, somehow they looked strange. We found him by a little bunker, protected from the wind. He wasn't wearing shoes. Auschwitz in the winter without shoes

"Reb Aharon, where are your shoes?"

"I traded them in for a candle."

"Please, Reb Aharon," we begged, "don't do it. They'll kill you."

"Listen," he said clearly. "This is Chanukah. On Chanukah, Jews light candles. That's what we do. The Chashmonaim weren't afraid; why should we be."

He took out a little pencil-thin candle, made the blessings, and lit it. We all stood there, frightened, yet excited. Who ever dreamt that one small flame could give so much light? But there was a tension in the air, a feeling telling us to run.

Then, suddenly, a German soldier comes walking out of the night. In one hand he held a whip, in the other, a pistol.

"Who lit that candle?" he barked at us. Reb Aharon stepped forward.

"I lit it," he said.

The German whipped him across the face. "Blow it out!" he yelled. "Blow it out!"

The Penny Candle

Reb Aharon just stood there. He didn't move. He didn't even lower his eyes. Then the Nazi took out his gun and shot him. That was it. He killed him right on the spot. We stood in fear, not believing our eyes.

"You," he shouts at one of my friends, "drag him this way." He dragged poor Aharon through the snow into the darkness. The German walked away, but you know, he forgot to blow out the candle, it was still burning.

Now, you won't believe me when I tell you this, but it's true, I saw it myself. The next night when we walked by the place Reb Aharon was killed, we looked over at the small candle – it was still burning, flickering away in the darkness. It lit up such a flame of hope in us. "Do you see it?" we asked each other. "Do you see it?" We all saw it. The candle was still burning.

INTEGRATION

And He said... walk before Me and be whole.

– Genesis 17:1

ONE OF THE SIGNIFICANT LESSONS I LEARNED from R. Dovid Din was the importance of normalcy in religious life. He himself seemed far from normal. He was an ascetic, a scholar and a mystic. He was a brilliant thinker, yet could nullify his consciousness and enter deep states of *devekus*. At the same time, he was married and raised a family. Enlightenment must be grounded in reality and grow out of a healthy, normal life, he would stress. Anything that "sticks out" or draws attention to itself is likely to be an expression of the ego. This applies even to spiritual experiences.

And yet, it's hard to stop yearning for them.

The Milk of Miracles

We are born with a taste for miracles, raised on fables and legends from the Bible. As children, we drink in these stories like milk. They feed our imagination, and nourish us with a sense of wonder and endless possibility. Even as we get older, the taste for miracles never leaves our mouth, and few things are more enthralling than stories of saints and wonder-workers, of inexplicable healings and sudden experiences of enlightenment. Such tales gives us hope, that no matter how bleak a situation may be, a miracle is always possible and can occur at any moment.

Judging from the many such events recorded in Scripture, it would seem that most miracles serve the same purpose – to produce a sudden deliverance, whether for an individual or a nation: Daniel in the lion's den, the splitting of the Red Sea, the sun standing still over Gibon. In a hopeless situation, God intervenes to change the course of nature and save those who trust in Him. These stories are then passed on from generation to generation. The entire evening of Passover – the holiday of redemption – is dedicated to recounting the miracles and plagues that accompanied the exodus from Egypt.

However, according to classic Jewish sources, the primary purpose of a miracle is not its redemptive quality but its revelatory nature. God is not limited to the miraculous to achieve His purposes, and can equally accomplish His will in hidden ways, for "the heart of a king is in the hand of God" (Proverbs 21:1). Miracles are more important for what they teach than for what they accomplish. The Hebrew word for miracle is *nes*, which also means "a sign"; for miracles are signs of a higher reality. The purpose of a miracle is not just deliverance, but a transformation in the consciousness of the one who experiences it. For at the moment of Divine influence, not only are the laws of nature transcended, but human consciousness itself experiences an unfolding. Thus the verse says, "You shall tell in the ears of your son, and of your son's son, the things I have done in Egypt, and My signs which I have done among them; that you may know that I am the Lord" (Exodus 10:2). That is, the signs performed in Egypt were meant to produce in us a knowledge of God.

Thus, there are miracles in the physical world, and miracles of the mind. Whenever a person has a spiritual insight, a moment of inspiration, or a peak experience that deepens his appreciation of life, he is experiencing a type of miracle. His sudden inspiration is a *nes* – a sign of a greater reality. Miracles such as these break through our normal perception and lift us to a higher level of consciousness. They awaken in us a closeness to God, and a desire to transcend the limitations of our physical existence.

Nevertheless, there is a problem with miracles, as well. At the moment of the miracle, God suspends the laws of nature and the limited consciousness of the human mind, but because this influence is imposed from without, when the miracle ends, the presence of the Divine is soon forgotten. Nature – human nature included – returns to its course, and a person must once again struggle with his own unrefined character, in a world which conceals God's presence. The classic Biblical example of this is the sin of the Golden Calf. Only forty days after the revelation at Sinai, the Children of Israel had already forgotten God and fallen back into idolatry. For, while miracles can spark the soul, they cannot guarantee change.

This explains Judaism's ambivalent attitude toward miracles. Although the Talmud records various wonders that happened to the sages of the time, it also expresses reservation about such occurrences. "Do not rely on a miracle," the Rabbis said, and "The fewer miracles the better." The Talmud tells the story of a poor man whose wife died, leaving him with an infant son that he was unable to feed. God performed a miracle and his breasts began to give milk like a woman's. "How great is this man, that God did such a miracle for him," commented one of the sages. "No, how unfortunate is he," a later sage concluded, "that God had to change the order of creation for his sake."

What is the order of creation? That growth occurs slowly, painstakingly, in proportion to our efforts. For only change that comes from below, born out of our struggles and aspirations, has lasting value. Though it may be less dramatic than a miracle, the transformation it effects can be permanent. Furthermore, by acknowledging those areas in our lives that need improvement, and working to repair the broken pieces of both self and world, we must, of necessity, involve everything around us in the process, thereby refining and uplifting the world. This is not a "moment of grace" but a complete reintegration of every aspect of life, and a perception of Godliness that grows out of the most fundamental reconstruction of the consciousness.

This same distinction is true of inner miracles – moments

of inspiration and enlightenment. I learned from one of my teachers that whenever a person has a "spiritual experience," though it may be powerful, the chances are that it has not yet been integrated into the being, for an "experience" is not the person himself, but something imposed from without. Too often it is a self-conscious form of enlightenment, and rarely does it last. On the other hand, when a person works hard on himself, though the process may not "feel" spiritual, when he grows, he does so as a whole. His experience is generated from within, not from without. In this case, the greatest growth is precisely that which a person may be least aware of.

Of course, miracles exist. There is a Kabbalistic principle that every spiritual journey must begin with a revelation – a miracle – that inspires and motivates our growth. This is like a father teaching his child to walk. God holds our hands and shows us miracles; the clearest sign that we are being helped from above. However, God also wants us to walk on our own, and soon hides His guiding Presence. Then we must proceed with faltering steps. This is reflected in the history of the Jewish nation. In its youth, it witnessed the miracles of the exodus and the desert journey. As the verse says, "On the day that you were born, your navel was not cut, nor were you washed in water for cleansing… nor swaddled at all… and I swore to you, and entered into a covenant with you, says the Lord God, and you became Mine" (Ezekiel 15). But as time passed, the miracles were hidden and the nation had to progress on its own, to learn the difficult job of serving God in the Land.

We all long for miracles, for the sudden inspiration that will fix our lives and the world. We are like the child of that poor man in the Talmud, nursing on the milk of a miracle:

The Milk of Miracles

When will we grow up? For no miracle can replace the work we must do ourselves. Only the most dedicated and mature effort will bring both ourselves and the world to perfection. God says, "Let us make man" (Genesis 1:26). "Us" – that is, God and man himself, for the work depends upon the both of us.

The Midrash says that "the world cannot exist without miracles." For they provide us with inspiration, and remind us that the Kingdom we are trying to build is ultimately not our own. However, true growth is never a gift from Above, but the result of a long and arduous process. In the end, we can achieve the transcendence that we desire, but only by overcoming the most difficult obstacles. The greatest miracle of all is that a person can change.

The Maggid's Coin
A children's story

There once was a poor Jew named Yaakov. He lived in a small town in Russia with his wife and five children. Try as he may, he found it almost impossible to make a living. He had no job, and absolutely no success in any venture that he undertook. There was never enough food in his home, and his children were always hungry. Their clothes were torn and dirty, the roof leaked, the floor creaked, and a heavy air of poverty hung over the house day and night.

One day, he and his wife were talking.

"My dear husband," she said. "I have heard that in the town not far from here, there lives a great Tzaddik – the Maggid of Ternovitz. Why don't you travel to see him? Ask him for a blessing. Perhaps he will bless us with a livelihood, and our situation will improve."

"But I can't afford a wagon," replied Yaakov. "I will have to walk."

"God will speed your way," she replied. "Go, and come back with good news!"

Yaakov packed some food and a few things he needed and set off on the road. He had been walking for some time, when a Jewish farmer with a wagon-load of hay passed by.

"Where are you going?" the farmer called.

"Ternovitz," answered Yaakov.

"Climb on, then," the farmer cried. "I'm going there too!" Yaakov climbed onto the back of the wagon. He took out a small Book of Psalms and started reading from it. After a short while, the farmer passed another man walking alongside the road. The man also climbed onto the wagon and started talking to Yaakov.

"*Sholom aleichem!* My name is Kalman. Where are you going?"

"I'm going to Ternovitz, to the great Maggid," Yaakov replied.

"The Maggid! I've heard of him. Why are you going there?"

"I'm hoping he will give me a blessing for livelihood."

"Can he really give you that blessing?"

"Don't you know?" Yaakov answered, "A Tzaddik can give blessings to whomsoever he pleases. All the store-houses of heaven are open to him."

"If I ask him for a blessing for wealth, will he give it to me too?" the man asked.

"If he wishes," replied Yaakov. "He can bless you with whatever he desires."

"Then I am going with you for a blessing," the man concluded.

The two men rode on in the wagon, speaking lively about Tzaddikim, miracles, and God's wondrous Torah. After a while, they passed another man walking besides the road.

"Moshe, Moshe," Kalman cried out. "Come with us, we are going to the Maggid of Ternovitz to get a blessing for wealth!" The third man climbed onto the wagon, and joined the other two in their discussion. A little while later, they passed a fourth man, walking along the road. "Shmuelik, Shmuelik," Moshe and Kalman cried." Come with us, we are going to the Maggid of Ternovitz." The four men rode along, sharing stories and food, and speaking about the greatness of the Maggid, and all the things they would do when he blessed them with wealth.

After many hours of traveling, they arrived in Ternovitz. The wagon-driver let them off in front of the *shul*. The four men entered the building with trepidation. They approached the *gabbai* and requested an audience with the Maggid. The *gabbai* went into the Maggid's study for a minute, then opened the door and ushered them in. The four men walked in and started trembling. The Maggid was sitting at his desk. He was as pale and thin as a candle, yet his eyes glowed like flames. An air of holiness surrounded him, and the room seemed filled with spiritual light. The men were speechless; they could not open their mouths.

The Maggid spoke first. "You must know that God gives a Tzaddik dominion over Heaven and earth. Everything is in his hands: wealth, poverty, wisdom and enlightenment. Whomever he blesses is blessed, and whomever he curses, cursed. I know why you have come, and I agree to help you." He opened his drawer, took out four coins and laid them in a row on the table.

"Each of you is to take a coin," he said, pushing them slightly towards the men. "You have permission to spend it on whatever you like. For on whatever you purchase, my blessing will descend. May God help you spend it wisely." The men each took a coin from the desk.

"One more thing," the Maggid said. "One small piece of advice. Think twice before you spend it!" The Maggid gave a slight gesture of his hand, as if dismissing them. The *gabbai* opened the door, and the men backed out of the room, thanking and blessing the Maggid as they left. Outside the *shul*, they jumped in the street with joy. Each one held his coin as if it were a diamond. "A blessing from the Maggid! A blessing from the Maggid!" they cried.

They set out on the road back to their homes, each of them lost in thought, imagining the fortune that would soon be his. As they walked, they passed through villages and towns, markets and orchards. Wherever they went, their eyes fell on the various merchandise, looking for the right item to buy, one upon which the Maggid's blessing would descend. In one particular market, they passed a Russian peasant selling a large horse.

"I have an idea," Shmuelik announced. He went over to the Russian and started bargaining over the price of the horse.

"I want to buy this horse," he told his fellow travelers. "What do you say?"

"It's a great idea," Kalman and Moshe told him. "Buy it, buy it!"

But Yaakov was not so sure. "Wait a minute," he said. "Let's think about it a moment."

"Aah, what's there to think about?" Shmuelik snapped. "It's a great idea!" Shmuelik bought the horse from the Russian, and when he paid him, he included the Maggid's coin.

"Well, I'll see you back home," he said as he climbed onto the horse. "There's no need for me to walk!" Shmuelik snapped the reigns, and the horse started off at a trot. He rode across the countryside, his mind already making plans for the future.

"As soon as I get home, I will ride to the palace of the baron. I'll tell him that I have the fastest horse in the country.

He will give me messages to deliver, and I will become his private courier. Soon I'll expand my operations and deliver messages for all the other noblemen in the land. I'll become so successful that I will buy other horses. Then I will purchase wagons and carriages to run from town to town. I'll have my own stables and pastures. I'll raise thoroughbred stallions that will become the most sought after horses in Russia. The Czar himself will buy his horses from me!"

And as he rode, the blessing of the Maggid descended upon the horse.

Suddenly, the horse started to run. Faster and faster it raced across the countryside. "Stop! Stop!" Shmuelik yelled. "Whoah! Whoah!" He pulled at its reigns, he kicked at its sides. The horse ran on as though a fire was coursing through its veins. "Help! Help! STOP! STOP!" Shmuelik cried. The horse ran across fields. It ran up hills, through forests. Shmuelik bounced up and down wildly. He hung on for dear life. Suddenly, the horse cut across a field and jumped over a low wall. Shmuelik went flying off its back and crashed onto the ground. "Ooowww!" His head hurt him, his arms hurt him, his legs and back hurt him. "Oh, Oh, Oh!" he groaned. He couldn't even move. Meanwhile, the horse kept running, and disappeared into the distance.

Of course, he never saw that horse again, nor did he see the Maggid's special coin, nor did he see any sign of blessing.

Yaakov and the two men continued on their journey, all the time considering things to buy. As they walked along, they passed an orchard. Sitting beside it was an old lady selling apples, which were big, beautiful and red.

"Wait a minute!" Moshe announced. "I have an idea." He went over to the old lady and asked her the price of the apples.

"I'm going to buy these apples," he declared to Yaakov and Kalman. "What do you think?"

"It's a great idea," Kalman told him. "Buy them, buy them!"

But Yaakov was not so sure. "Wait a minute," he said. "Let's just consider the matter a moment."

"Aah! What's there to consider? It's a great idea!" Moshe bought a large box of apples, and asked the old lady if she would sell him her wheel-barrow, too. She agreed, and put the apples in the barrow. When he paid her, he gave her the Maggid's special coin.

"It will take me much longer to walk home with these apples," he told his two friends. "You two go ahead without me. I'll see you back in town." Yaakov and Kalman set off alone, leaving Moshe to slowly push his wheel-barrow forward. As he walked, he began to make plans for the future.

"As soon as I get home, I will have my wife cook all of these apples into pies and cakes. We will sell them around town. They will be so delicious that people will come to us for more. I will buy more apples, and fruits and nuts. We will bake other cakes and pastries. Soon we will open a large bakery. People from all the surrounding towns will come to buy from us. We will make challah and rolls, cakes and pies. I will buy my own mill to grind the flour, and wheat fields to grow my own wheat. I will have land, and farms and hundreds of servants."

And the blessing of the Maggid descended upon the apples.

Moshe looked at those apples glistening in the sun. They seemed so crisp and delicious. "I think I will just try one of them," he thought. He took an apple, made a blessing, and bit into it. Mmmm! He had never tasted an apple so sweet, so delicious. It tasted like the fruit of *Gan Eden!* He walked a little further. "You know," he said to himself. "I think I will just try another." He took another apple and ate it. It was so tasty, so scrumptious, it tasted like the *bikurim* – the First Fruits that the Jews would eat in Jerusalem on the holy festivals. He walked a bit further. "Just one more…" he thought. Well, it wasn't long before he sat down on a rock and ate and ate and ate, until he had finished off the entire crate of apples. He lay on his back on the ground, his stomach as bloated as a watermelon. "Oy, Oy, Oy!" he moaned. "I can't move! I feel sick!" He lay there on his back the rest of the day, and half the night too.

Of course, he had no more apples, nor did he have the Maggid's special coin, nor did he see any sign of blessing.

Yaakov and Kalman continued on their way. In every town and market they passed, they would pause to consider the different merchandise. On the outskirts of one town, they passed a large farm with many chicken-coops outside. Dozens of chickens ran around in the yard – it was the town slaughterhouse. As they walked past the farm, Kalman glanced through an open door.

"Wait a minute," he said. "I have an idea. Come with me." The two men walked inside. The room smelled strongly from chickens. There was blood and dirt on the floor. In the middle of the room was a *shochet* holding his knife. At a table beside the wall, an old lady sat, plucking out the feathers, preparing the chickens for market. Beside her, were several large boxes filled with feathers. Kalman called over the *shochet*. "What do you do with all these feathers?" he asked, pointing to the boxes.

"We sell them to people to stuff pillows and blankets," the *shochet* replied.

"I'm going to buy these feathers," Kalman said to Yaakov. "Isn't that a good idea?"

"I'm not so sure," Yaakov replied. "Let's think about it for a minute."

"Aah! What's there to think about? I say it's a great idea!" He turned to the *shochet*. "Give me all the feathers that are in this box," he said. "And find a bag for me to put them in."

The *shochet* ran into another room and returned with a large sack. They stuffed the bag full of feathers and twisted it closed. Kalman gave the *shochet* the money, and with it, the Maggid's special coin. He flung the sack onto his back, and he and Yaakov set off on the road again. It was starting to get dark, but they were already close to home. As they walked, Kalman was already lost in his thoughts of the future.

"As soon as I get home, I will have my wife sew a dozen pillows and blankets. We will stuff them with these feathers. Then we will set aside a special room in our house for guests. Whoever passes through town will stay with us. When they curl up under our warm blankets, they will have such a good night's sleep that they will want to come back. Soon, everyone will want to stay with us. We will buy a bigger house and turn it into an inn. All the noblemen and lords will stay there. We will open a tavern and make our own beer and wine. Soon we will be hosting princes and kings. We will buy other inns throughout Russia. Then we will buy land, and build houses, mansions and palaces!"

And the blessing of the Maggid descended upon the feathers.

Suddenly, the big sack of feathers started to feel so warm and cozy, so comfortable and snugly, that it was making Kalman tired. He just wanted to curl up underneath it and take a nap. He had never felt so sleepy before in his life.

"I'm so tired," he said to Yaakov. "Can we just sit down and rest for a few minutes. I'd like to take a nap."

"You want to rest now?!" Yaakov said. "We're almost home. Can't you wait a little while?"

"Oh no, I'm so tired. I must lie down."

"You do whatever you like," Yaakov replied, "but I'm not waiting for you. I'm going ahead." Yaakov kept walking. Kalman stepped off the road into a field. He found a grassy spot beneath a tree and lay down. He curled up under the sack stuffed with feathers, and tucked one corner under his head for a pillow. In a moment, he had fallen into the deepest, most comfortable sleep he had ever felt, lost in dreams about all the money he would soon be making.

But as he slept, he let go of the sack, and the feathers began to spill out. The wind started to carry them away, and they drifted up into the sky, across the field, and into the trees. They looked like thousands of tiny white moths fluttering in the moonlight. As the feathers slipped out, Kalman's head sunk lower and lower, lower and lower, until... Clunk! His head hit the ground. He awoke with a start. He felt the sack, it was empty! He jumped up in shock. The feathers were blowing across the field in every direction. "Oh no! Oh no!" he cried. He went running after them trying to catch them, stumbling and tripping in the darkness. But the wind just blew them away. In the end, all he had was a handful of feathers, and an empty old sack.

Of course, he never saw those feathers again, nor did he see the Maggid's special coin, nor did he see any sign of blessing.

Yaakov was almost home. As he passed the familiar farms on the edge of town, he started to walk faster and faster. He was anxious to get back to his house. He put his hand in his

The Maggid's Coin

pocket and felt the Maggid's special coin. He was so happy! He couldn't wait to show his wife. He walked through the main street of town. It was late. The lights were out in all the houses, and everyone was asleep.

Suddenly, a man stepped out of the darkness and walked over to Yaakov. It was a wandering beggar. The man put out his hand. "*Tzedakah*, Mister, *tzedakah?*"

Yaakov stopped and put his hand in his pocket looking for some change. He checked his pants' pocket and his jacket, but they were all empty... except for the Maggid's coin.

Yaakov thought once.

"Oh no, I'm not going to give him this coin. This is the Maggid's special coin. My entire future depends upon this coin. How can I give him this coin?"

Then, he thought twice.

"But how can I not give it to him? Look at this poor fellow. His clothing is so torn. His shoes are falling apart. He looks so thin and sad. He needs it more than I do." So Yaakov gave him the coin.

And the blessing of the Maggid descended into his own heart.

And Yaakov's heart filled with love for the Jewish people, and compassion for all of God's creatures. He felt the pain of the poor and the suffering of the needy, and longed dearly to save them from their misery. From that moment on, Yaakov's life changed. He dedicated himself to helping and giving to others. His house was always open to whoever needed a meal, and he gave of everything he had: money, food and time. He accepted the suffering of others as if it were his own, and spent all his days helping Jews, wherever they were. When God saw all the good that Yaakov was doing, and how he only wanted to help His holy people, He blessed

Yaakov's home with all manner of goodness. Yaakov found success in everything he did, and his family never lacked anything again. Their lives were dedicated to helping others, and their home was a place of kindness and charity to all who passed their way.

> A soul descends into this world for seventy or eighty years and goes through whatever it goes through, all for the sake of doing another Jew a favor – materially, and all the more so, spiritually.
>
> BAAL SHEM TOV
> *Kesser Shem Tov, hosafos 130*

GOALS

*To do Your will, my God, I desired,
and Your Torah is in my heart.*

– Psalms 40:9

AS OPPOSED TO VARIOUS EASTERN RELIGIONS, which stress passivity, equanimity or the idea that "you are already there," Judaism is very purpose-driven (except on Shabbos). This is reflected in the concepts of national and universal redemption, and on the personal level, with the constant drive for self-improvement. The Kotzker Rebbe once said: "The time for eating is when you are a child. The time for resting is when you are in the grave. And as for depression, there is no time for that at all."

In writing the following piece, I remembered a statement of the German Poet, Goethe: "Energy is the basis of everything. Every Jew, no matter how insignificant, is engaged in some decisive and immediate pursuit of a goal... It is the most perpetual people of the earth...."

Seeds of Vision

*P*urpose is God's gift to a fertile soul. It is a vision of what can be, that originates in the future and moves backward in time, not pushing a person to do great things, but pulling them there, at times by force. And when it is planted in the hearts and minds of men and women, it leads them to give birth to a reality immeasurably greater than themselves.

The great Chasidic master, Rabbi Nachman of Breslov (1772-1810), explained this as follows:

> Everything has a purpose, and this purpose has another purpose, one more exalted than the next. For example: The purpose of building a house is for a person to have a place to rest. The purpose of resting is to have strength to serve God, and the purpose of serving God…
>
> Now, the final objective of each thing is more closely connected to the original thought than the thing itself from which the goal derives. The goal is also closer to thought than the thing is, and from the goal, the deed evolves.

Every journey towards a goal begins with a vision. But this final purpose, which stands at the end of a long chain of smaller steps, is actually closer to the original intention than all the stages in-between. For example, explains Rabbi

Nachman, when a person desires to build a house, before the plans are even laid and the first nail driven in, an idea of the house stands complete in his mind's eye. It is from this final aim that all the necessary steps to attain it will be derived. In this sense, the goal is closer to the initial vision than any of the steps taken to reach it. This vision is a spark of the future embedded in the present. When it enters the heart, it directs all of a person's life and desires towards its attainment. In this way, the future draws the present towards itself.

This implies that our greatest dreams exist not only in the future, but can be found in the present as well. All things bear a faint reflection of their ultimate goal, and a person with a sense of purpose views the world differently than others. Though he stands at the beginning of a long sequence of events, he already imagines the end. He does not merely see the seeds in the apple, but the apples inherent in the seeds. He sees the warm home already present in a lumberyard of bricks and boards, and the image of God in the raw materials of our lives. For some, a purposeful life manifests itself as a drive for personal greatness. For others, their sense of purpose is intertwined with the good of the community. Still others are concerned with the future of the entire world. Likewise, communities, nations and even entire civilizations bear an innate, often unspoken, sense of purpose, which underlies all of their laws and customs. In all cases, a person of vision lives in both the present and the future. He embodies the mystical teaching that God "wedges the end in the beginning, and the beginning in the end."

Purpose, then, has deep esoteric roots. According to the Kabbalah, the first emanation of the universe, the initial movement of the Divine from out of Itself, was an act of

Will, or purposefulness. Into a womb-like space created by God in His own Being to hold the universe, a drop of Divine effluence descended to form the world. This "drop" is the creation in its perfection, as it arose in God's mind. Yet, as it descended through the worlds, it became increasingly clothed in materiality, until its Divine origin was obscured. Nevertheless, in the root of creation it remains in its purity. It is this point of Will that motivates all existence in the slow and steady ascent to its source.

Metaphysical formulations such as this one are not mere expressions of some mythic cosmology; they seek to articulate fundamental processes underlying all existence. For instance, there is a point deep in every human being where the soul touches God; where, beneath our personal desires and opinions, the Divine Will for each individual shines forth. Were this point to be revealed, it could illuminate the entire world and drive a person inexorably towards his or her fate. However, more often than not, this point is obscured, and its noble goal absconded by meaningless distractions or self-centered goals. Even then, it is never silent, but throbs with the undeniable sense that there is a higher purpose to life.

On the microscopic level too, the power of purpose can be found in the blind race of the sperm cell to reach its goal, reflecting the irreducible human desire to *become*, to lose oneself in order to bring to birth something infinitely greater. It is not merely a biological process that drives this cell onward; it is the future individual already present in its genes. The promise of what can be that is hidden in what is. And though months and years will add flesh and bone, thought and emotion, this primal drive to transcendence remains forever hidden in the recesses of the human consciousness – pushing, motivating – even when its original source can no longer be remembered.

Finally, society too has a goal and a purpose. It is conceived of in the minds of great men and women, who inscribe their visions in scriptures and constitutions, and whose words are meant to grow in the heart of a people, until they give birth to a nation that reflects the holy aspirations of its founding fathers. Here, too, the higher power beneath these words must never be forgotten; for societies, no less than individuals, can stray from their goals, and come to embody false and meaningless values and ideals.

This understanding of purpose explains why great achievers so often feel that their accomplishments are not their own. For, indeed, their vision does not originate with them – it is the future itself lodged in their hearts that drives them on. Furthermore, in the long and arduous process of actualization, they must constantly face their own limitations and shortcomings. But it is precisely these repeated trials that force them to turn to God in prayer, in the hope that His Will will move through them for Its own ends. This paradoxical combination of single-minded determination on the one hand, and utter humility and dependence on the other, is what moves mountains. As the Chasidic saying goes, God alone can fix the world using broken tools.

Countless obstacles stand between a vision and its actualization, and the process of coming to realization is fraught with challenges and frustrations. Rarely is something worthwhile achieved without having to overcome major obstacles, and bringing an aspiration to birth is often so difficult that the visionary may lose sight of the goal and be ready to give up. Here, one needs a mother's wisdom (as opposed to a father's inspiration); for a child grows hidden in the womb, with only the vaguest shape perceivable from without. But the mother knows well that it is there; she has felt it from the beginning. And she knows that eventually it *must* be born. So too, it is not enough to be inspired by a lofty goal; one must remain faithful to it in one's heart despite all obstacles, until it is ready to emerge.

This, then, is a call to educators and leaders: To cultivate the ground, to plant the seeds, to instill a sense of purpose within every individual and on every level of society. Especially in our youth, whose fields of heart are moist and fallow and in which every seed of hope takes instant root. And though not every dream will sprout to fruition, it is a precious time that must not be lost. Yet there is a widespread pessimism among our youth today, a fear that our civilization, our very species, may perish before reaching its goal. As a result, many people, young and old alike, abdicate the pursuit of higher goals in exchange for transient, self-centered pleasures: Sterile gods that will not give birth.

Yet the present is pregnant with the future, and we must not let the pains of labor make us forget the child that is being born. Can anyone perceive the infant growing in the womb of our civilization? Can anyone even envision it in adulthood? Do we remember any longer what we are building? Society's educators and leaders must instill in their charges a noble vision of the future, but more than that, they must teach them how to maintain this vision even during the challenges that will arise in the process. For a difficult situation is nothing other than a womb for our dreams, and a life of purpose means being a midwife to the future. Humankind is created by God for a purpose, and we must not let the vision die a stillbirth.

It is difficult enough to remember our individual purposes, let alone the purpose of humankind. Yet, there are people in this world who have the whole future of our species turning in their guts, robbing them of sleep, taking away their appetite. Their pain is the very struggle of humanity to give birth to a better future, to God's own vision for us. A better world will only be built by individuals who can see it already in the present, though it appears as only the smallest seed of hope. Rabbi Nachman taught that the greater the vision, the greater the obstacles that will arise to obstruct it, yet it is God Himself who places these obstacles in our path in order to increase our desire for the goal, for without this desire, we would never continue. We must live life backwards – a child is born head down into the world – and we must have faith that the One who created us will bear us and carry us.

> Shall I come to labor and not give birth? says the Lord. Shall I who causes birth shut up the womb? says your God. Rejoice you with Jerusalem, and be glad with her, all you that love her; rejoice for joy with her, all you that mourn for her. That you may suck, and be satisfied with the breast of her consolations; that you may drink deeply with delight of the abundance of her glory. For thus says the Lord: Behold, I will extend peace to her like a river, and the wealth of the nations like an overflowing stream, and you shall suck thereof: You shall be borne upon the side, and shall be dandled upon the knees. As one whom his mother comforts, so will I comfort you; and you shall be comforted in Jerusalem. And when you see this, your heart shall rejoice, and your bones shall flourish like young grass; and the hand of the Lord shall be known toward His servants... (Isaiah 66:9-14)

The purely righteous do not complain about evil, rather they add justice.

They do not complain about heresy, rather they add faith.

They do not complain about ignorance, rather they add wisdom.

R. AVRAHAM YITZCHAK HAKOHEN KOOK
Arpilei Tohar p. 39

"I was young and now I have grown old, yet I have never seen the righteous forsaken or his children begging bread." (Psalms 37:25)

How is it possible that King David never saw a righteous person and his children abandoned, even once in his life? We read and hear about such occurrences every day.

Rather, what he was saying is, "In my entire life, *I* never saw such a thing. Because if I ever saw a righteous person and his family suffering or in need of support, I immediately ran to help them and alleviate them of their troubles.

RAFAEL YITZCHAK EPHRAIM ESTRIN

Counting Back the Minutes

The great Chasidic Rebbe, Rabbi Dov Ber of Radoshitz, was traveling across the Polish countryside. Night fell, the roads would soon be unsafe, and so he directed his wagon driver to stop at the first Jewish inn along the way.

In a short while, they had pulled up in front of a small tavern. The owner greeted them warmly, helped them with their bags, fed and watered their horse, and prepared for Rabbi Dov Ber a special room reserved for traveling rabbis and noblemen. After praying the evening prayer, Rabbi Dov Ber retired to his chambers and to bed, tired after the long day's journey.

Soon the house was quiet, the fields outside still. Only the occasional barking of a lone farm-dog broke the silence of the night. And yet... the clock on the wall... it was ticking in the most amazing way... it wouldn't let Rabbi Dov Ber sleep. He tossed and turned in his bed. He got up and started pacing the room. Verses from the Books of the Prophets flooded his mind, songs of deliverance and hope. He tried to lie down again, but the clock kept ticking, forcing him to rise from his bed once more. Thus he spent the entire night, pacing his room in anxious anticipation.

In the morning, the tired but exhilarated rabbi approached the inn-keeper. "Where did you get that clock in the room?" he asked.

Counting Back the Minutes

"That clock? Well, several years ago another rabbi stayed in the room, Rabbi Yosef of Turchin, the son of the Seer of Lublin. He came for only one night, but the weather turned bad and he was forced to stay for several days. In the end, he did not have enough money to pay the bill, so he covered the difference by giving me that clock. He said that he had inherited it from his father."

"Now I understand why I couldn't sleep," said Rabbi Dov Ber. "Most clocks in the world cause only sorrow, for they count the hours that have passed – another day gone, another opportunity lost. But the clock of the holy Seer of Lublin counts the time that is coming – another minute closer to the final redemption, another second nearer to the age of universal peace."

The Midnight Ride
A true story

It was too late. Too late to be standing by the side of the road hitching for a ride. Too late to catch the last bus from Har Nof to the center of Jerusalem. Too late to go to bed and get up on time for morning *seder*. Dovid Feldman stood a few feet away from the curb, his hand wearily outstretched in the traditional Israeli hitchhiker's sign, and watched the cars speed by. "Please, somebody, stop," he whispered "Don't be scared of me. I'm a Jew!"

Moments before, he had closed his *gemara* and left the *beis midrash*, after spending several extra hours reviewing his studies. But the last bus had already passed, and now he was stranded. His only hope was to catch a lift. Dovid leaned against a parked car, opened a *sefer* and tried to read a little by lamplight, but his attention kept wandering back nervously to the road. A cool, midnight breeze drifted over the mountaintop, and his thoughts turned inward. As his eyes followed the headlights of the oncoming cars weaving down the highway, he took stock of his day.

"It was a good day," he assured himself, "I made it to yeshiva on time, and even learned a *parshah* of Chumash on the Number Eleven bus. Morning *seder* went well. I took only one coffee break, (or was it two?) I cut my lunch hour short to get back to learning. The *shiurim* were good, and, *Baruch Hashem*, I have good *chavrusos* here." He shifted uneasily from foot to foot, and glanced far up the road. "What's missing?" he thought. "Why this constant feeling of dissatisfaction? Why don't I have enthusiasm for Torah study?"

A cool breeze of a memory floated into his mind, words of admonition he had heard from many teachers in the past. "You are not living up to your potential," he heard them say once again. "You could do much better if you tried." It was the same old dilemma, a complaint leveled against him since childhood. Nor was it his problem alone. The vast majority of humanity, so he thought, fails to live up to their potential, even those who try. The Vilna Gaon said that Hell's greatest torture lies in showing a person what he or she *could have* been.

"But what can I do? How can I realize my potential?" he mused. "Perhaps I should get up a half hour *earlier* in the morning and not waste so much time in the *mikvah*. And that second cup of coffee has got to go." As he stood considering his options, a prayer slowly formed on his lips. "Please God," he beseeched, "I want to succeed in Your holy Torah. I want to do Your *mitzvos*. I don't want to waste my life. Please help me live up to my potential."

Dovid was still repeating these words when a car pulled up in front of him: a sporty, red BMW. He got in the front seat and fastened the seat belt. The driver was a young, Sefardic man, dark skinned, clean shaven, sporting a stylish haircut and a small velvet *kippah*, cocked slightly to the side of his head. Dovid eyed the dashboard: it was decorated with cartoon stickers and idiotic sayings. He considered the fuzzy dice that hung from the rearview mirror and the hand-shaped amulet, inscribed with Hebrew letters to ward off the evil eye. "So much for potential," he thought, "This guy is far from *avodas Hashem*." But then he reconsidered. "On second thought, God did send him to give me a lift. Maybe He sent an answer to my question, as well."

"Tell me," he asked his host, "how does a person live up to his potential?"

The driver answered immediately. "*Bitachon* – trust in God!"

It was a good answer, and Dovid was pleased at how quickly the driver had responded. If a person truly trusted in God, how much more could he apply himself to his endeavors. How much less time would he waste needlessly, and how much calmer would his mind be to devote himself to his studies. As Dovid considered this answer, the driver spoke again.

"Take me, for example. I live in Givat Shaul. Every night I wake up at midnight and drive to the gravesite of Rabbi Mordechai Sharabi, the famous Kabbalist. He's buried on Har HaMenuchot. Have you been there? Then I say these ten Psalms." He pulled out a small pamphlet of Breslover Chasidus from the glove compartment. On the back was written, "Recite these ten Psalms. They are a wonderful remedy for all your ills."

"It's dark and deserted there, but I have trust in God that I will be safe, and so I'm not afraid."

Dovid was amazed. This simple Jew was rising each night, going to the grave of one of the holiest Tzaddikim of the last generation, and reciting *Tikkun HaKlali*, the profound *segulah* for *teshuvah* revealed by Rabbi Nachman of Breslov. So much for Dovid's casual, deprecatory assessment.

A few minutes later, the car pulled up on the corner of Kiryat Moshe and Givat Shaul. "This is as far as I go," his host told him, "Be well, and I hope you find your potential." Then he drove away.

Once more, Dovid stood by the side of the road with his hand outstretched. Across the street, bright lights shone through the doors of Angel's 24-hour Bakery. The smell of fresh pastries filled the air. Dovid reflected upon the driver's response – trust in God. It was a good answer, yet, for some reason, it was lacking, as though it were only half a solution. However, now was not the time to consider the issue further. The only thing that mattered was getting to bed. If Dovid didn't get another lift, he would have to go the rest of the way alone, an infinitely long twenty-minute walk.

"Oh, God, I'm so tired. I have no more strength. Please, please, send me a lift." The words had barely left his mouth when an old, white Subaru pulled up. A thin, Yerushalmi chasid, with a crushed felt hat, long, unkempt *peyos*, and a straggly beard, beckoned him in. Dovid sat quietly as they drove to the center of town. He thought about his day, about his potential, about trust, about bed, and he was pleased that God had so quickly answered his prayer for a lift. His driver, too, was silent, and neither said a word.

As Dovid stepped out of the car, he felt the need to share at least one word with his host. He turned to the driver and said. "Thank you so much for picking me up. Do you see God's kindness? Just when you pulled over, I had been praying, 'God, I have no more strength, please, send me a lift.' And then you stopped!"

"If you had no more strength," the driver replied, "why did you pray for a lift? You should have prayed for strength! A person should always pray for the main thing, not the secondary one. Pray for the *ikkar*, not the *tafel!*" And with that, he sped away.

Dovid was stunned, as though the words had been spoken to him by a prophet. Not only was this an answer to his question, it was an answer to his answer – a commentary on the reply he had previously received.

What does it mean to have trust? Is it merely a matter of doing more than before, or making a greater effort? Trusting in God *is* only half the answer. If we are to fulfill our potential, we must also trust in ourselves.

Each person comes into this world for a specific task and is blessed with special gifts, and no two individuals will ever be alike. The famous Chasidic Tzaddik, Reb Zusia of Anipoli, once exclaimed, "When my life is over, and I stand before the Heavenly Court, I am not afraid that they will ask me 'Zusia, why weren't you Moses?' But I am afraid they will ask, 'Zusia, why weren't you Zusia?'"

God, too, desires that each of us fulfill our potential. But to do this, we have to know where our potential lies, in order to pray for the main goal in life, and work to actualize it. Then God will surely guide our development. If not, we may waste our lives without ever finding satisfaction. If we recognize our strengths, however, then our lives and our *avodas Hashem* will be filled with joy and enthusiasm.

Reb Nosson of Breslov writes: "Rabbi Nachman spoke at length about the great differences between the Tzaddikim of the previous generation – the disciples of the Baal Shem Tov and the Maggid of Mezritch. One Tzaddik would travel across the countryside and speak in public, another would remain in his town. One would pray before the congregation slowly and with cries of devotion, while another prayed in a whisper. This one devoted his time to Torah study, and this one to charity and saving Jewish lives. Nevertheless, they all

The Midnight Ride

came from one Rebbe (the Baal Shem Tov), and there was a great love between them. Each one served God according to the root of his soul and it was impossible for them to be alike. God's greatest delight is that He has so many Tzaddikim and good Jews in the world, each giving Him special pleasure not found in the next. This is the meaning of the verse: "Israel, in whom I am adorned" (Isaiah 49:3). Jews embody a whole spectrum of colors. God does not make the same thing twice. Each individual has his own path according to the root of his soul in the Supernal Will."

Everyone has some idea of what his or her unique potential may be. A person's heart may be drawn to a particular type of Torah study, or certain *mitzvos*, or a particular style of *avodas Hashem*; this is not accidental. Only, one needs the courage and the trust to pursue this path, and to seek out teachers and friends who recognize the validity of his way, and who will help him develop it further. Above all, a person should never be apologetic because he finds himself drawn to a mode of worship different from that of others.

> Just as a person has to believe in God, so he has to believe in himself. That is, that God cares about him, and that his deeds are not worthless and transient. Rather, he should believe that his soul comes from the Source of Life, may He be blessed, and that God delights in him, when he does His will.
>
> R. Tzadok HaKohen of Lublin
> *Tzidkas HaTzaddik* §151

~ FAITH ~

*Do you know what is beyond the clouds,
the wondrous works of Him who
is perfect in knowledge?*

– Job 37:16

IN 1994, I WAS LIVING IN THE ARZEI HABIRAH neighborhood of Jerusalem. It was around that time that the city built "Road One," known today as Hayim Barlev Boulevard – an intra-city highway that separates east and west Jerusalem. The road also runs past some *chareidi* neighborhoods, and cars use it on Shabbos. I remember lying in bed on Friday nights and hearing the young *chareidi* men shouting angrily at the passing cars, "Shabbos! Shabbos!" until late at night.

I couldn't sleep. Not because of the noise, but because I was distraught over the lack of tolerance and compassion that I was hearing. The question I asked then – and still ask now – is, is this the goal of a religious life? Is this an expression of faith and love of the Creator?

It was around that time that I wrote the following piece.

Dweller on the Plain

There is a city of the mind, with uniform streets and secure borders, with rigid laws and strict legislation, whose like-minded citizens share every goal and opinion. Beyond the city limits is a wasteland. On a barren plain where no man should live, the stranger dwells. And though he cannot enter the city, he is its greatest threat.

Every human being is an inhabitant of this city; each person lives within boundaries that define and limit his perception of reality. The borders that divide one individual from another may be drawn on many grounds: religious, nationalistic, ethnic. They may be the viewpoint of a particular individual, or the shared vision of an entire community. They may shift over time, or remain constant. In all cases, what lies within the borders is an entire world-view, with its own internal logic, absolute truths, social mores, dreams and aspirations. Conceptual underpinnings fortify the position. Frequent battles – both verbal and physical – charge it with emotion, until the surrounding barriers become almost impenetrable, and the world is divided into those within and those without. Even when the borders are very broad, there is always someone beyond them – that person is the stranger.

The Hebrew word for "stranger" – *zar* – is also the root of the word "border," for the existence of strangers is predicated upon the existence of borders. Whether it is an individual, a nation, or an alien philosophy, the stranger stands outside the borders of our perspective, on a dark plain beyond our range of vision. He embodies a position ulterior to our own. And because his existence contradicts our definition of reality – upon which our sense of self is built – he presents a threat to our very being. The more dogmatically we cling to our beliefs, the more dangerous the stranger becomes – and the more strictly the borders of our perspective must be patrolled.

Often, in an attempt to diminish this threat, society will define the stranger as sub-human, deserving of bigotry and hatred. At best, he is avoided. At worst, he becomes subject to attack; strange ideas become subject to burning. Such has been the experience of the Jewish people throughout their long exile, as it has been the experience of all minorities and those who dwell on the fringes of society.

Yet the stranger continues to exist. He demands our attention. As long as we fail to acknowledge him, our vision of reality will remain incomplete. Spiritual growth is the process of venturing beyond one's boundaries into unfamiliar terrain. There one learns a deeper truth, which can only be born out of the encounter with the unknown.

According to the Kabbalah – the Jewish mystical tradition – at the heart of creation lies a paradox; it is the paradox of God and the world. On the one hand, God is Infinite, One and Whole, utterly transcendent of time and space, lacking nothing. Yet, He emanates a creation that is finite, temporal and dualistic – the very opposite of His intrinsic nature. Upon this dichotomy, Kabbalistic teachings build a deep understanding of God's relationship to creation.

According to the Kabbalah, it should be impossible

for the world to exist in the overwhelming Presence of the Absolute. Thus, God's primary act of creation is the establishment of a border between His Infinite Being and the universe. Were it not for this boundary, all existence would be nullified and absorbed in the Divine Light. This division is the metaphysical root of all subsequent borders: those between nations, between individuals, and within the human mind. As the verse says, "When the most High divided to the nations their inheritance, when He separated the sons of Adam, He set the boundaries of the peoples…" (Deuteronomy 32:8). God's Infinite Presence is described as "surrounding" creation from the outside. Within itself, the universe appears to be an independent system: integrated, harmonious, operating according to its own natural laws. Only rarely does God actually cross this line. A miracle, for instance, occurs when the Creator extends Himself into the boundaries of the universe to disrupt the fabric of reality. Even then, it is only "the finger of God" that is revealed (Exodus 8:15) – the smallest indication of His power. Thus, a border is drawn between us and our Maker. The Infinite is on one side, and we are on the other.

This means to say that the ultimate stranger to creation is God Himself; for His Being is ultimately antithetical to our own. Were He to reveal Himself fully, creation would cease to exist. Traditional Jewish sources make it clear that the various names and descriptions of God found in Scripture and liturgy are in no way meant to limit or define His actual Being. They are for our sake alone, allowing us a means of relating, in our terms, to the transcendent Source. As for God Himself, the verse says, "No man can see Me and live" (Exodus 33:20). A direct encounter with the Absolute will always be a terrifying experience, for it negates our very existence, just as fear of ego-annihilation is the greatest obstacle on the path to enlightenment.

And yet, there is a deep desire in the soul of every living being to go beyond the boundaries of private experience and become part of a larger whole. Nonetheless, when we look beyond the border of all our words and prayers, our vision fails us. Human eyes cannot behold infinity. A path across this boundary does exist, but it depends upon the development of a different kind of vision.

At the heart of the religious experience is the mystery of faith; for where knowledge ends, faith continues. On the simple level, faith is an inner certainty in the existence of a greater reality. On a deeper level, it is an alternative form of knowledge, one that transcends the boundaries of the intellect. In the language of mysticism, faith is a boundless experience, an extension of the being into the darkness, beyond the borders of human perception. Jewish texts often speak of faith in terms of night. "It is good to give thanks to the Lord... to relate Your love in the morning, and Your faith in the nights" (Psalms 92:2-3). Faith is a dark knowledge, lacking the bright light of the intellect. Spiritual growth is the process of cultivating this inner faith to the point where one crosses the boundary between God and creation, and understands that somehow the two are not antithetical. Outwardly – rationally – the borders continue to exist, but on the inner plain, God ceases to be a stranger.

So too, with the strangers of this world. It is only through a deepening of the spirit – that takes us beyond the platitudes and dogmatism of our beliefs, into a relationship with the Divine – that enables us to accept the presence of the stranger, even when he does not conform to our own definition of reality. Seeing with faith is as though seeing through God's eyes. "My eyes are on the faithful of the land," says the Almighty (Psalms 101:6). It means seeing a world in which everything has a place, and even the stranger is not outside of the Divine will. For God embraces everything, and gives life and existence to all. "Do not belittle any person," says the Talmud, "nor despise anything; for every person has his hour, and everything has its place." God is the "place" of the universe; for He makes space for all reality, and allows all things to be. He cares for the needs of each one of His creatures, and there is nothing outside of Him. He alone sees the whole picture, in which everything has its place.

Thus it is that by acknowledging the stranger we acknowledge God. For the encounter with that which exists beyond our understanding forces us to deepen our definition of reality and transcend the limitations of our personal beliefs. Even as we maintain our position, we come to recognize the intrinsic worth of the other – that in every person is the image of God, and in every opinion, a point of truth. Accepting the stranger means living in a world of paradox – where the presence of the other is validated, even though it does not fit into our vision of reality. A world in which God exists, even where He logically cannot. For, the Divine Unity is not compromised by the existence of creation – it extends to include it. Although God transcends the world, the world is not antithetical to Him. There are no strangers to God.

Ultimately, spiritual realization is the experience of paradox, living at once within and beyond one's borders. The point is not to erase all boundaries. Judaism sees the establishment of laws as the very basis of an enlightened and harmonious society. Religious transformation, as well, depends upon both discipline and creed. On the personal level, it is precisely an individual's boundaries that give definition and meaning to life. And at the very root of creation, the division between God and the world is necessary for our continued existence. Borders must exist – the point is not to be limited by them. We must develop the vision to see beyond them.

Every person lives within boundaries – afraid to venture into the darkness beyond. But what is there to fear? "And Moses stepped into the darkness, where God was" (Exodus 20:18). When we behold the world with the eyes of faith, there are no more strangers. God's presence can address us from anywhere, and every encounter becomes a setting for revelation. The world becomes a place of wonder – of paradox – which is the fundamental principle of creation. Slowly, our vision clears, and we come to recognize the One who transcends all boundaries – seeing Him with eyes that are no longer foreign. "That I might see Him for myself; that my eyes might behold, and not a stranger's" (Job 19:27).

> "Where is God?" the Kotzker Rebbe once asked. Then he answered, "Wherever you let Him in."
>
> R. Menachem Mendel of Kotsk
> *Emes v'Emunah*

Simchas Torah of the Chazon Ish

It was close to midnight on the evening of *Simchas Torah*. Rabbi Avraham Yeshaya Karelitz, the great "Chazon Ish," Torah leader of the previous generation, was leaving the Ponovezh Yeshivah in Bnei Brak. Although advanced in years, he had sung and danced with all his might, in joy over the Torah. As he walked home with his students, he saw a man sitting on a bench weeping openly. The man was clearly a religious Jew, but his dress and appearance seemed foreign to that neighborhood.

"My dear friend, what is wrong?" the Chazon Ish asked him gently.

The man was startled by the Chazon Ish's presence. "Rebbe," he cried, "I'm so lonely! I am a convert to Judaism and don't know anyone in town. I feel that I do not belong, and that there is no place I can go to celebrate over the Torah."

The Chazon Ish thought for a moment. "My friend, if you will sing, I will dance for you."

The man began to sing – quietly at first, then louder. He sung of his love of Torah, of God and of the Jewish people. And there, in the middle of the street, the Chazon Ish began to dance. As the man's voice rose in joy, the Chazon Ish danced with ever more beauty and grace – back and forth across the sidewalk, his hands outstretched, as a man dances before a bride and groom. Slowly, a crowd of people gathered to behold the sight – the leader of the generation dancing before the convert. Finally, the man stopped singing.

"Bless you, Rebbe. You have restored to me my soul."

> This is the ultimate compassion – that no flaw or transgression, no severity or other quality, can withhold God's continual goodness to man. So too, nothing in the world – no sin or improper act – should keep a person from giving to those who depend upon him. And just as God sustains all creatures, from the highest to the lowest, despising none of them (for if He despised any creatures because of their insignificance, they could not exist for even a moment), but watches over them and bestows upon them His compassion, so a person should give to all, and despise none. He should respect even the smallest creature and give it his attention, bestowing his goodness upon all who need it.
>
> R. Moshe Cordovero
> *Tomer Devorah, chapter 2*

The Souvenir

A true story

The sun rose harshly over the Sinai Desert. Its crimson rays struck the shattered remains of an Egyptian bunker, waves of heat spread over the bodies of the young Israeli soldiers, strewn about in the sand, like weeds. An unearthly silence gripped the scene. It was hard to believe that only hours before, this had been the scene of the fiercest battle. Now the Egyptian outpost was taken, its soldiers were all dead, and the remnants of an Israeli troop lay sprawled out on the sand, shutting their eyes against the light of the rising sun. The Yom-Kippur War raged on every border of the land. This battle, the Israelis had won.

Only Ronen Mizrachi was wide awake. He fixed his eyes on the blue expanse above and dug his fingers slightly into the sand. He knew that he was alive, though he did not know why. The battle had been the worst he had ever experienced. He had been sure that he would be killed. But here he was, with the remnant of his platoon.

As he lay there staring up, an unusual feeling began to stir within him, and something like a desert breeze began to blow across an empty place in his heart. A growing sense of exultation and a feeling that something – Someone – way above had spread forth His hand and protected him during the previous night's battle. This powerful feeling lingered for a moment, as if looking for a suitable place to alight, but Ronen, the child of a secular kibbutz, a stranger to even the most basic tenets of the Jewish faith, lacked the words to capture the sensation. He had never once prayed in his life, and so now, he merely observed the feeling as if from afar – until it slowly faded away. He would have said something, had he only known the words.

The soldiers began to stir, and slowly, one by one, they rose and shuffled toward the charred Egyptian bunker. They were looking for souvenirs. After such a battle, a soldier cannot return home empty-handed. He must have something to show his parents and friends: perhaps an Egyptian army knife, or an officer's signet ring, or a decorative medal.

But Ronen was uninterested. He lay quietly in the sand and watched as the feeling of exaltation slowly faded away. Then suddenly, he rose and walked quickly toward the bunker, anxious now to find something to fill his surprising inner emptiness, something to show his friends back home and tell them about the battle he had won.

In the bunker, everything was burnt and bloody. Ronen's eyes scanned the bodies of the dead Egyptians for a souvenir, but his friends who had preceded him had taken everything of value.

Suddenly, he noticed a bulge in the breast pocket of one of the dead soldiers. "A pack of cigarettes will have to do," he thought. But when he unbuttoned the pocket, he found a small book written in Arabic. "Great! This will be my souvenir," he said, and pocketed the book without a second thought.

Back at camp, he showed the strange book to his friend,

Amir, who read Arabic. Amir laughed, "Do you know what this is?"

"Of course not," Ronen replied. "Is it something special?"

"Ronen, you found yourself a Koran!" Amir laughed as he tossed the book back to his friend. "Use it in good health!"

Ronen returned the book to his breast pocket. So what if it was a Koran, he thought. Even better! Now he can tell his friends how he took a holy book from the pocket of a dead Egyptian.

Days went by, the war dragged on, yet the strange feeling of emptiness did not leave Ronen's heart. He would lie awake on his bed at night thinking about his life, considering subjects that had never before entered his mind – God, fate, the purpose of life. Ideas for which he did not even have the words. At those times he would take out the small Koran and flip through it at random. The foreign script meant nothing to him, yet the book itself told many stories. He would rub the cracked leather cover, examine the various pages: here was one more thumb-worn than the rest; here the Arab had underlined a certain word; here he had written a note in the margin; here something wet had fallen on the page and blurred the text. "That Egyptian believed in something," Ronen would think to himself. "But what do I believe in? Nothing."

The war continued, more battles, more victories. One morning, as the convoy crossed a desert plain, they suddenly came under a barrage of enemy gun fire. The soldiers threw themselves to the ground and responded with their machine guns in the direction of the enemy. There was a moment of silence, and then an Israeli soldier called out: "Cease fire! We have him." A lone Egyptian gunman rose from behind a sand-dune. Tall, thin, blood streaming from his forehead, he raised his hands high above him and walked slowly toward the soldiers in a gesture of surrender. Amir ran over to him with his pistol drawn. "He's okay," he shouted. "We've got him! Take him to the personnel carrier."

There were about thirty men in the carrier. Ronen was in the far corner and they sat the Egyptian on the floor beside him. The man was dazed and confused. Ronen eyed him suspiciously. He opened his canteen and offered the Egyptian a drink. "Take water!" he said. The Egyptian took the cup with trembling hands and drank its contents in one gulp. "He's so thirsty," thought Ronen as he poured him another cup. The man blessed Ronen in Arabic – he blessed his father, his mother, until ten generations back. Ronen gazed at the Arab with a mixture of hatred and pity; the Arab kept his eyes on the floor.

There was something bulging in the Arab's breast pocket, a suspicious object. "Take that out," said Ronen with a gesture and a nudge of his rifle-butt. The Arab reached into his pocket and slowly pulled out a small leather-bound book embossed with Hebrew letters – a Jewish *siddur*.

Ronen stared in disbelief. His mind raced wildly. A thousand thoughts flew through his head. Then slowly, instinctively, he reached into his own breast pocket and removed the Koran. The Arab stared in disbelief as he read the words on the cover. He looked at Ronen, their eyes met – two worlds, two cultures, two enemies – yet at that moment, speaking the same language. Ronen looked at the *siddur* and understood. He understood how the prayer-book had fallen into Arab hands; just as the Koran had fallen into his. And he understood something of Heaven's ways – that Providence has many messengers. And he knew what to do next. He stretched forth his hand and gave the Arab the Koran, and the Arab gave him the *siddur*. The Arab put the Koran in his pocket, and Ronen looked down at the prayer-book in his hand. He opened it to the first page and read the words: "I give thanks to You, living and eternal King, for You have returned my soul to me with compassion; Your faithfulness is great."

And at that moment, something opened up inside of him. The heart that had been empty for twenty-one years; that had longed to leave the Land of Israel after the war in search of excitement; that had scorned the religious life but found nothing better in its place – the heart opened up with a cry and a shout that rang across the desert like cannon fire.

That prayer was only the beginning. The *siddur* gave Ronen the vocabulary he never had. As the days went by, he turned to it more and more. It spoke to his heart; it brought tears to his eyes. Prayer led to understanding, understanding to Torah, and slowly, to a return to the religion of his forefathers. It was a souvenir that held more memories than he could imagine – memories of the distant past, and of hope for the future.

Ronen never did leave Israel. After the war he entered yeshivah. Eventually, he married and settled down to build a Jewish home. Today, the *siddur* sits on the bookshelf in his study, a souvenir of the most important battle he has ever won.

COMPASSION

The Lord is good to all, and His compassion
is on all that He has made.

– Psalms 145:9

A FRIEND OF MINE WAS GOING THROUGH A VERY difficult period. After two divorces, he was depressed and broken-hearted. He sought advice from various Rabbis in Jerusalem, and found that they generally addressed his situation in one of two ways: either they admonished him or they tried to comfort him. Neither approach really helped, however. Finally, he went to speak with R. Boruch Shochet, the Karlin-Stolin Rebbe – a man known for his great brilliance and clarity. My friend poured out his heart to the Rebbe, who listened intently, and then offered a single comment: "I see you enjoy talking about your problem."

My friend was shocked. The Rebbe's answer cut through all his layers of self-pity and illusion. He had put his finger exactly on the problem itself.

We often think of compassion as the goal of spiritual work. But compassion may not always manifest itself the way we expect it. The greatest compassion someone can offer us may lie in cutting through our illusions.

Writing Between the Lines

One of the hardest things in the world for a writer to do is show compassion; for it is the very opposite of his craft. This is because writing is about conveying ideas, and as soon as an author sits down to work, an image of his readers comes to mind – an audience that he knows well, whose expectations and preferences he has encountered before. Thus, before the creative process even begins, a writer may find himself limited by the very people he is addressing. For each word is born into a community – the shared assumptions of writers and readers that stretch back long before the present exchange – and in addressing a specific topic, an honest writer finds that there are only two choices before him: to say something that affirms his readers' previous knowledge or to say something that challenges it. In either case, the writer threatens his readers with death – from the right or from the left – unless, somehow, he can write down compassion itself.

According to Kabbalah, every phenomenon can be understood according to its position on the Tree of Life, the map of the *sefiros* – the ten primary emanations through which God directs the world. Thus, the ten utterances of creation, the Ten Commandments, and the ten plagues all correspond to different *sefiros*, and knowing the place of each thing on the Tree, and how it interacts with other *sefiros*, reveals much of its essential nature.

The Tree is divided into three columns. On the right are the *sefiros* of expansion: *Chochmah, Chesed* and *Netzach* - Wisdom, Loving-kindness and Eternity. On the left, are the forces of restraint: *Binah, Gevurah* and *Hod* - Understanding, Strength and Majesty. And in the center, the line of balance and unification: *Kesser, Tiferes, Yesod*, and *Malchus* - Crown, Harmony, Foundation and Kingship. Compassion is associated with the *sefirah* of *Tiferes*, which mediates between two contrasting forces. *Chesed*, to its right, is effluent, and implies the act of giving, regardless of the worthiness of the receiver. *Gevurah*, to the left, represents the power of restraint, which withholds goodness even in the face of need; for according to strict justice no one is ever deserving enough. Compassion, mediating between the two, implies giving, but always in accordance with the needs and limitations of the receiver.

But writing is all about *Chesed* and *Gevurah*, and every sentence is invariably a statement of yes or no. When an author tells his readers something that they already know, he is showing them *Chesed*, and merely reinforcing their previous beliefs. He is not challenging them. Yet, like a mother's love, this can smother the reader and constrain his or her growth. If a writer is aware of this problem (though many are not), he may try to do the opposite - to write with *Gevurah* and confront his reader's assumptions. Yet, here too, compassion is lacking, for the readers may very well be offended by the words, and close their minds to them. And even if the reader does heed them, the writer has still not transcended the underlying framework of prior assumptions. He is merely elucidating the dark side of the reader's beliefs, which was always there in potential; for every affirmation contains its own negation, every yes implies a no, every *Chesed* has its hidden *Gevurah*: "These are the generations of Isaac, the son of Abraham. Abraham gave birth to Isaac" (Genesis 25:19).

Let us see how these ideas apply in practice, using compassion itself as a subject.

As we know, compassion may be the single most important trait on the spiritual path – the very essence of enlightenment. On the verse, "You shall follow after the Lord your God… and to Him you shall cling" (Deuteronomy 13:5), the Talmud asks, "How can one follow after the Divine Presence; it is a consuming fire?! Rather, follow after His attributes. Just as He is gracious and compassionate, so you should be gracious and compassionate." Compassion is not just another virtue; it is the chief means of attaching ourselves to God. Rabbi Nachman of Breslov went as far as saying that God's whole reason for creating the universe was to make a place in which He could reveal His compassion. This applies to creation as a whole, and to each of its details, so that everything – from dust-motes to supernova – bears its specific shape precisely according to the amount of Divine compassion it has the capacity to reveal.

On the other hand, compassion can also be one of the most crippling of traits. The Talmud states that "a person with compassion has no life." This doesn't refer only to emotional life, but essential life – spiritual life. Because a person with too much compassion, who is too preoccupied with the welfare of others, will have no time left for his own spiritual growth. He will never study, never pray, never meditate. Nothing will become of him. "Only a person who is as cruel to his family as a raven (which is said to abandon its young), can ever truly acquire Torah," says the Talmud. Progress on the spiritual path not only requires cruelty to oneself, and the denial of many of life's basic comforts and needs which impede the spiritual quest; it demands cruelty to others, as well. The Talmud tells the story of Rabbi Adda bar Matna, who abandoned his wife and family in order to study Torah. "What will happen to the children?" his wife asked him. "Are there no more herbs in the marsh for them to eat?" he replied. These are hard words. But there is simply no way a person can come close to God without first knowing how to turn his back on others and their misfortunes.

Now, is there compassion in these words about compassion? No, there are merely two sides of an issue: *Chesed* and *Gevurah*. Pleasant words that affirm the value of compassion, which we already know, and harsh words that deny its validity and are painful to hear. Words on the right and words on the left. Yet even the most disturbing words are still within the realm of the known, for they merely contradict our previously held beliefs.

There has yet to be a word of compassion written on this entire page.

It seems to me that if writing is to be truly compassionate, it must not merely transmit information, but must free both writer and reader from the bonds of the predictable, of the known. To do so, however, it must partake of a higher level of compassion, which transcends even the limitations of this craft.

According to Kabbalah, the *sefirah* of *Tiferes* has another attribute – that of Truth. "Give truth to Jacob (*Tiferes*), kindness to Abraham (*Chesed*)" (Micah 7:20). For truth is the greatest compassion that one human being can possibly show another. Not the truth of "true or false," but that which transcends the world of duality altogether. Truth always enters our lives unexpectedly, cutting between yes and no, between the pleasant and the disdainful, neither affirming nor denying, but engaging us in a moment of absolute being – of Presence.

It is known that the ten *sefiros* also correspond to the ten holy Names of God. *Tiferes*, embodying truth and compassion, corresponds to the holiest of them all, the YHVH, the Tetragrammaton itself. This name, which seeks to convey God's very essence, is a unique construct of the verb "to be," and can be said to mean "Eternal Being." For being *is* truth. It is the only truth worth conveying, and to confront someone truthfully, with all of our being, always transcends the division of yes and no.

But can writing ever convey such truth? The very act of writing is nothing but *Chesed* and *Gevurah* – the affirming or denying of a thought, the expansiveness of the paper versus the narrowness of the pen, the yes of the white and the no of the black. Can a writer ever put himself so much into his words that presence emerges from between them? The Ten Commandments begin, "I am the Lord your God." In Hebrew, the first word, I – *Anochi*, is an acronym for the words, *Ana nafshi ketavit yehavit* – "I gave My soul over in writing." For in writing His holy book, God gave over His very Essence, so that His words are true, compassionate, and eternally present. Can a human author emulate God in this as well? Can soul be conveyed in writing?

Rabbi Nachman says that beneath each written letter, at the interface of ink and paper, there is a color that is neither black nor white, but the union of them both. It is called *techeles*. According to Rabbi Nachman, this corresponds to the Hebrew word *tachelis*, which means "final goal or purpose." For just as the physical meeting-point of pen and paper is the goal of the act of writing, so there is something beneath each written word that reflects the ultimate goal of human searching – a truth beyond all yes and no, a glimmer of the Oneness that underlies this world. It can be revealed, perhaps, but only when an author comes to the realization that there is nothing more he can say.

There comes a time in every creative endeavor when the artist must lose his vision, the author his voice – then it becomes painfully apparent that if left to himself, he will *never* produce anything new, but will be forever trapped by the limitations of his craft. At that moment, there is nothing left for the writer to do but retreat from the page, from the imaginary reader who so entices him. In the language of mysticism, it is a moment of ego-annihilation. For just as the mystic's painful experience of the duality of this world forces him to seek reconciliation on a higher level of reality, so the writer's inability to truly communicate something new forces him to draw inspiration from a deeper source. It is a painfully frustrating moment – a feeling of impotence – but it is indispensable; for only when space is made for a higher force to enter the creative process can something new be born. "There are three partners in the creation of a child," says the Talmud, "the father (*Chesed*), the mother (*Gevurah*), and the Holy One, Himself." Only in the space between *Chesed* and *Gevurah* can words truly come alive.

If the writer can pass through these straits, if he can humble himself to the source of inspiration, then his words take on a different tone, for they express the soul. Words like these can cross all boundaries, as the Sages have said: "Words that come from the heart can enter a heart." For no two things can ever unite – neither pen and paper, nor writer and reader – unless space is made for something higher to enter between them. And only in that moment of union does it become apparent that the reader never really constricted the writer, as had originally been felt, but the other way around: the writer's own initial preconceptions and lack of honesty limited not only himself, but his reader's perspective as well; whereas words of the heart are fresh, new, and bring freedom and inspiration to all who encounter them – writer and reader alike.

Can compassion be conveyed in words? Can words wake us up and evoke in us something higher? "Can these bones live?... O Lord God, You know!" (Ezekiel 37:3). According to Kabbalah, every human being is also a letter, and every family unit a word. On our city streets, in our homes and offices, sentences are being written, lines in a book that only God can read. Can we find compassion there, too? Can Presence emerge from beneath our feet, and "truth sprout from the ground" (Psalms 85:12)? Can we together form words that say more than yes or no, but convey presence and compassion?

Perhaps.

Black Fire on White Fire

In Europe, there were two childhood friends that went to yeshivah together. They were inseparable. They played together, studied Torah together, and served God together. Time passed, and as they grew in their Torah knowledge, it became clear that they were both destined to become great Rebbes.

And so it was.

One became the Vorki Rebbe – Rabbi Yitzchok of Vorki, and the other became the Rebbe in Trisk – Rabbi Avraham, the Trisker Maggid.

They made a promise to each other that every week, no matter what, they would write to each other. In fact, among the chasidim, it was a great honor to deliver the letters each Friday afternoon. Finally, one chasid was chosen to carry the letters back and forth between the Vorki and the Trisker Rebbes. He dared not miss a week, lest another chasid jump in and take his place.

Friday morning the Vorki Rebbe would hand the chasid an envelope. He would carry it through the woods, reach Trisk about midday, and wait for a reply. Usually, within half an hour the response was ready, and he would carry it back to Vorki.

This went on week after week, year after year. In fact, our story begins after this had been going on for almost fifteen years.

The chasid was carrying the letter to the Trisker Maggid. Suddenly, in the middle of the forest, a *ruach shtus* – a foolish thought – entered his mind. "You know, I have been carrying these letters back and forth every week for fifteen years now. I wonder what is written inside...."

But to open the Rebbe's mail... whoever heard of such a thing! So he put it out of his mind and delivered the letter. Yet the thought kept nagging at him.

The next week, the chasid took the letter from his Rebbe, the Vorki Rebbe, and started on his way through the forest to the town of Trisk.

"I really wonder what they have to say to each other. After fifteen years of writing every week, what could they possibly say? But to open the Rebbe's mail!"

Yet the chasid could not help himself. He stepped off the path into the thick of the woods and with trembling fingers opened his Rebbe's letter.

It was blank – a blank piece of paper. "What's going on here?" he thought. "Can it be that I have been carrying a blank piece of paper back and forth for fifteen years?"

The chasid was beside himself, but he had to deliver the letter and so he did.

After about 20 minutes, the Trisker Maggid gave him his response and the chasid set off for Vorki. Once again, in the thick of the woods, he stepped off the path. With trembling fingers, he opened the Trisker Maggid's response.

It was a blank piece of paper.

The chasid felt like he was losing his mind. But what

could he do? Soon it would be Shabbos and he had to return home.

He could barely rest that Shabbos, his thoughts kept plaguing him. At the Friday night *tish*, he could hardly look at his Rebbe sitting at the head of the table. And the whole following week, his mind was in turmoil.

The next week again he stepped off the path –
A BLANK PIECE OF PAPER!

"*Gut in himmel* – God in heaven! What is this? For fifteen years I've been going back and forth, in the cold, in the rain, to deliver blank pieces of paper. These people are supposed to be Tzaddikim! These people are supposed to be holy! Is this how they have their fun? Torturing a poor chasid for fifteen years! I must talk to the Rebbe about this. But how can I tell him that I opened his mail?" That Shabbos was a Shabbos from hell. The chasid was so tortured… "How can I go on… but how can I tell the Rebbe…?"

By Saturday night it was too much.

"Rebbe, I have to talk to you. I must ask your forgiveness, but I have to talk to you.

"Rebbe, for fifteen years I have been carrying your letters to the Trisker Maggid. After all that time, well, two weeks ago I opened your letter and I found a blank piece of paper. I did it again last week and again found a blank piece of paper. Rebbe, I am so embarrassed that I opened your letter, yet I am so troubled that you would ask me to carry a blank piece of paper back and forth for so long."

The Vorki Rebbe, who was known for his great love of Jews, looked gently at the troubled chasid. "You needn't be so upset – many times, in the course of those years, I did send you with regular letters, and yes, sometimes with a letter that was totally blank. Let me explain.

Black Fire on White Fire

"It says in the Holy Zohar, our book of mystical knowledge, that in heaven, the Torah is made of black fire written on white fire, and that the white fire is holier than the black fire.

"The black fire is, of course, the letters of the Torah and the white fire is the parchment. How can the Zohar say that the white fire - the parchment - is holier than the black fire - the letters? It is the letters that make up the Torah itself!

"Let me explain. There are two kinds of relationships one can have with Judaism.

"One relationship is definable. I am connected to Judaism because I know this information about Judaism. I understand this truth about Judaism. I like this or that *mitzvah*.

"The other relationship is indefinable. I am Jewish because I am infinitely connected to being Jewish. I cannot explain it in words, yet I feel it with every aspect of my being.

"The letters of the Torah - the black fire - represent a relationship that I can explain. Just as I can read letters, understand and grasp them, so too the relationship.

"Yet the parchment is the white fire. Just as the parchment is clear or white, boundless, without any definition, so too is my relationship with Judaism. It is there, it touches the depths of who I am, yet I have no words, no definition, to explain it.

"That is why the Zohar says the white fire is holier than the black fire, because the connection that one makes with Judaism - with other people - which is explainable and definable is not as deep or as sweet as the connections we make with Judaism, or with others, which are beyond definition.

"I grew up with the Trisker Maggid. We were childhood friends and went through a great deal together. We are deeply connected to one another. Sometimes I do write him regular letters. But sometimes, we just want to share with each other that we have no words to express how connected we feel – it is beyond words."

The First Lesson

There seemed little that young Mordechai's parents could do with their unruly son. They had tried everything to get him to stay in school – pleas, threats, and promises – but nothing seemed to help. While other Jewish children were busy studying the Torah, Mordechai was out playing in the shtetl streets. While the other children were opening their first page of Talmud, Mordechai was climbing trees. It was not his rambunctious behavior that troubled his parents, but his total lack of interest in Torah study. He was a bright child; how could he so forsake the occupation that had been the passion of his ancestors for over three-thousand years?

His parents were about to lose hope, when they suddenly heard that the famous Chasidic Master, Rabbi Aharon the Great of Karlin, would soon be visiting their town. Word of his remarkable piety and of his miraculous blessings preceded him. Surely, they thought, he could help them find a way to discipline their wayward son.

On the day of Rabbi Aharon's arrival, the entire village was abuzz. People lined up outside his lodgings to greet him and receive his blessings – for health, success, or livelihood. Mordechai and his parents stood in line as well. When their turn came, they were ushered into the holy man's chamber. Rabbi Aharon sat in his chair, his eyes were piercing, his face burned with the awe of God. The parents explained their situation.

"So, he won't learn Torah!" announced Rabbi Aharon in a frightening tone. "You two step out of the room. Leave him here with me. I'll teach him what it means to study Torah."

The parents were taken aback. Is this what they had wanted, to leave their son in the hands of this powerful figure? Still, with no other choice, they backed out of the room, leaving Mordechai alone with the rabbi.

Rabbi Aharon rose from his chair and sat on the couch. "Come here, my boy," he said in the gentlest of tones. Mordechai approached him. Rabbi Aharon took him by the hand and gently drew him to his chest. He held the child to his heart for a long time. Slowly, the boy began to relax, until he returned the embrace. Finally, Rabbi Aharon let him go, kissed his forehead, and went to open the door.

"You can take your son!" he practically yelled at the parents. "I've taught him what Torah is all about. He'll be a different child from now on!" The parents took little Mordechai and left.

From that day on, Mordechai's disposition changed. His love and dedication for Torah grew steadily. In a short time, he had surpassed all of his classmates. By the time he was a young man, he was recognized as an outstanding scholar. Eventually, he became a Chasidic Rebbe himself.

Often, when recalling his youth, he would tell his followers, "The first lesson I ever learned in Torah was when the great Rabbi Aharon of Karlin held me silently to his heart."

The First Lesson

It is impossible to love God through human effort alone, since love only exists between equals, and how can an axe pride itself to say it loves the woodchopper? However, God, in His endless compassion and love, calls the Jewish People "My sister. My undefiled. My twin" (Song of Songs 5:2), and tells us, "I have loved you with an everlasting love" (Jeremiah 31:2). And when God loves a person, naturally, that person will love Him back.

R. Tzadok HaKohen of Lublin
Tikanos HaShovim 5:5

When a person loves the Torah, the Torah loves him back and reveals to him all its secrets, like a beloved to her lover. Likewise, when a person loves the Jewish people, the Jewish people love him back, and reveal to him all the secrets hidden in their souls. Thus, Aharon carried "the names of the Children of Israel in the breastplate of judgment on his heart" (Exodus 28:29). For the secrets of their souls were revealed to Aharon – the lover of Israel – allowing him to know all the secrets of the world. When he would ask questions of the breastplate, the letters with the answer would protrude. Meaning to say, when a lover of Israel contemplates the names of the Jewish people, his heart swells in love; thus, he knows God's will for the world.

R. Tzadok HaKohen of Lublin
Tzidkas HaTzaddik §198

RETURNING

*...He devises plans so than none shall
remain outcast from Him.*

– 2 Samuel 14:14

THERE WAS A TIME IN MY LIFE THAT I WAS very pious. I sought a life of spiritual purity and closeness to God – as I imagined it to be. I was very strict in *halacha*, and very hard on myself. I threw away anything that I feared would sully my vision, including all my secular books and magazines.

It was an intense period of life, though not necessarily a happy one. But God did me a favor. For reasons beyond my control, I left Israel for America, where I eventually entered a Master's degree program at Yeshiva University. Suddenly, I was thrown into a world of broad ideas and universal values. And, I was quite happy.

Holiness is a wonderful goal, but being true to yourself is even better.

The Still Small Voice

There is a call that echoes in creation. It does not stop. It is never silent. It calls in a million voices, though it has only one source. It is heard in a million ways, though its message is always the same. It is a call to the Source. No matter where a person may be in life, the call reaches there. It is the single most insistent force in creation. It is the *reason* for creation; for the purpose of life is to know God, and the entire universe is merely a vessel through which God calls us back to Him.

> Now Moses kept the flock of Yisro his father-in-law, the priest of Midian: and he led the flock around the back of the desert, and came to the mountain of God, to Horeb. (Exodus 3:1)

At first, the call is imperceptible. It beckons so quietly that it is almost always heard as something else. Kabbalah speaks of creation as multi-dimensional, with one level hidden in the next. At the heart of them all is God. Likewise, the innermost longing of every individual is for God. But when this core desire is obscured, it takes on other forms. Chasidic writings speak of "fallen loves" – worldly desires as misguided longings for the Divine. What attracts us in the things of this world is never the object itself, but the spark of holiness within it, and the relationship with God that uncovering that spark implies. At every moment, we are searching for our Maker, even when we are unaware of it. "From the rising of the sun to its setting, My Name is great among the nations, and in every place incense is burnt and sacrifices are offered to My Name" (Malachi 1:11). In every place, taught Rabbi Nachman of Breslov, even those places where God is hidden.

Yet, it is from those very places that the call is first heard, for God addresses each individual in his own terms. One person may hear the call in the words of poetry or philosophy. Another may be aroused by the call of political ideals and social justice. Yet another, in spiritual practices, such as yoga or meditation. The call may sound in the Jewish soul with uniquely Jewish causes: the State of Israel, the fight against anti-Semitism. What is similar in all cases is that the person is uplifted and brought to a higher level of social or spiritual involvement. However, at this stage, the call is still indirect. It addresses us from behind, as it were, leading us "around the back of the desert to the mountain of God." Yet, even as we tend the flocks of Yisro, we may still be traveling towards Horeb. And if we keep listening, the call begins to reveal its actual source, the One truth that lies at the heart of our most noble endeavors.

> And the angel of the Lord appeared unto him in a flame of fire out of the midst of a bush; and he looked and, behold, the bush burned with fire, but the bush was not consumed. And Moses said, I will now turn aside and see this great sight, why the bush is not burnt.

For the true searcher, the world is ablaze with God's Presence. The Midrash relates that Abraham – the first spiritual seeker – beheld a lit-up palace. "There must be an owner of this palace," he concluded. Finally, the owner revealed himself to him. Creation spoke to Abraham. By contemplating its wonders, he came to recognize its "Owner." Rabbi Nachman said that the world is far from God only because people do not take time to think about their lives. Thus, the spiritual search begins when we turn aside from our mundane preoccupations and see the wonders in life and in creation. It takes only a slight turn for the call to reveal its true source. "Open for me a door the size of a pin-hole, and I will open for you the supernal gates," the Zohar quotes God as saying. A pin-size hole is enough to let God in, commented Rabbi Tzadok HaKohen, but it must pierce the heart entirely.

> And when the Lord saw that he turned aside to see, God called unto him out of the midst of the bush, and said, Moses, Moses. And he said, here I am.

Through this tiny opening, God's Infinite Presence floods in. The sudden realization that God exists, that life has a purpose beyond the meager values of the self, that there is a Presence in Creation infinitely greater and more profound than anything one had previously imagined, breaks into the consciousness like the ocean. It is a mighty call. "The voice of the Lord is in power. The voice of the Lord is in majesty. The voice of the Lord breaks the cedars" (Psalms 29:4–5). God's call now strikes the person with full force, for only such a powerful revelation can completely detach the seeker from the fallacious world-view in which he had previously been trapped.

> Moreover, He said, I am the God of Abraham, the God of Isaac, and the God of Jacob. And Moses hid his face; for he was afraid to look upon God.

At first, the call is indefinite – a general proclamation that the Creator exists; slowly, the words become more distinct. There comes a point in each individual's development when the relationship with God can no longer be based on personal feelings alone, but on commitment to the tradition – when "our God" becomes the "God of our fathers." Accepting a spiritual discipline is perhaps the most difficult step a seeker can take, for it means embracing a body of laws and customs that will forever separate one from the rest of the world. One may even try to deny this call, to hide one's face, but there is no avoiding the truth. God's Presence is strongly felt in the heart, and only the forms of the tradition can fully give it voice.

When the initial fear subsides, a passionate drive for holiness grips the seeker, and with it, a willingness to change. Beginning practitioners can be recognized by the determination in their eyes, the intensity of their worship, and their concern over even the smallest details of religious observance.

Beginning in the 1960s, an unprecedented phenomenon occurred in the Jewish world. Large numbers of young men and women from secular backgrounds began returning to the faith of their ancestors, to the laws and practices that their parents and grandparents had abandoned decades before. Religious outreach programs appeared on college campuses. Special yeshivos were founded to cater to these late beginners. The return to the Land of Israel flourished. These newcomers all shared a burning desire for God that had previously been seen only in the lives of the great Tzaddikim. The call of God rang so loudly in their ears that the world fell away. They abandoned their jobs, their goals, their secular world-view. They adopted new names, new modes of dress, of speech and of action. The same is true of every spiritual seeker. The beginning period is one of radical transformation, the previous lifestyle is discarded and a new religious persona takes its place. One's past seems only to be an impediment, while the future holds the promise of unlimited growth.

This initial period of grace may continue for several years, but it does not last forever. Slowly, the enthusiasm wanes, routine performance of *mitzvos* replaces the original intensity, the thunder of Sinai falls silent. For a time, the seeker may try to recreate the initial enthusiasm through his own efforts; but in his heart, he knows that he is fooling himself. Now comes a long period of darkness – the forty years in the desert. Now it is the seekers turn to call. God seems so far away. The seeker calls and calls; he can call his guts out, but not receive an answer. "I am weary with crying: my throat is dry, my eyes fail while I wait for God" (Psalms 69:4). This drama may unfold over the course of years, and it may repeat itself in miniature many times a day. There are brief moments of illumination, a sense of Divine closeness, a renewed hope for the future, only to vanish the very next minute, leaving behind boredom and despair.

But God is not truly far away. He is only silent for a moment, and is drawing the seeker close to Him even in concealment. One of the great obstacles on the spiritual path is pride, an intrinsic element of human consciousness since mankind succumbed to the Serpent's promise "you shall be like gods" (Genesis 3:5). When the soul is aroused by the call of God, invariably and at the same time, the shell of ego that surrounds it is also strengthened. Beginning seekers are recognizable not only by their fervor, but by an indefatigable conceit over their own spiritual accomplishments, and an often critical attitude towards others. By concealing His Presence, God allows the seeker to experience his own helplessness and insignificance. In the heart-breaking silence that follows, the seeker is humbled, the pride removed. Nevertheless, as the Kotzker Rebbe said, "There is nothing so whole as a broken heart." After all the crying, the calling, the beseeching God to return, what remains is the humble acceptance of one's limitations, a recognition of the truth, a "heart of flesh" (Ezekiel 36:26).

It is at the point when the seeker has been completely broken and can no longer deny his imperfections that God's call is heard once more, but now in a different tone. "And behold, the Lord passed by, and a great and strong wind rent the mountains and broke the rocks in pieces before the Lord; but the Lord was not in the wind: and after the wind, an earthquake, but the Lord was not in the earthquake: and after the earthquake, a fire: but the Lord was not in the fire: and after the fire, a still small voice" (1 Kings 19). It is not in the voice of religious intolerance or artificial enthusiasm that God ultimately speaks to us, but in the voice of humanity, love and compassion, that calls from every corner and aspect of life. This voice is never silent. It speaks to us in life's smallest encounters, and beckons us to relate to Him with all our most human emotions and foibles. Thus, the Torah, as a spiritual path, is especially concerned with the sanctification of the mundane, and the relationship with God that is born out of the most basic human needs and emotions.

And He said, Do not draw near: put off your shoes from your feet, for the place upon where you stand is holy ground.

In the beginning, God calls the seeker away from himself; ultimately, He calls him back to himself. When the fire dies down, the person returns to who he is, and in returning, finds God waiting. "Remove your shoes, for the ground you are standing upon is holy." When we remove the ego that stands between ourselves and the ground of our being, we can hear God's voice calling to us from even the simplest aspects of life. "The voice of my Beloved... Behold, He stands behind our wall, He looks in at the window; He peers through the lattice... let me see Your Countenance, let me hear Your Voice" (Song of Songs 2).

In returning to himself, the seeker rediscovers his own unique strengths, and the special gifts that God bestows upon each individual. Gifts that had previously been discarded as insignificant now become the very vessels through which God communicates to us. This is the meaning of the burning bush. The bush burned with fire, but it remained a bush. A person can burn with the presence of God, but remain human, remain who he is. Ultimately, God's call is a personal call, addressing each one of us, who we are, where we are, calling upon our strengths and humanity. "He heals the broken-hearted, and binds up their wounds. He counts the number of stars and calls them all by their names" (Psalms 147:3-4).

RETURNING

"And Judah drew near to him…" (Genesis 44:18)
   He drew near to himself.

R. Menachem Mendel of Kotzk
Emes v'Emunah §362

A person first entering the gates of Chasidus has a much sweeter experience than that of even the great Tzaddikim who are already inside. This is like a person who first enters a candy store. The shopkeeper, wanting to sell his merchandise, lets him taste a bit from the sweetest confections. But after the buyer has tasted everything and would like to try more, the shopkeeper tells him that he must pay. "At first, I let you taste everything so that you could know how good they are. Now that you like it, you must pay. I didn't treat you for nothing!"

The same applies to a person who enters the garden of Chasidus. God lets him taste from the hidden light. The person subdues his evil inclination, returns everything to the good. He gets a taste of *avodas Hashem*, and the pleasure of true prayer. But once he recognizes the sweetness of Chasidus, he must work hard, for that is the only way to acquire it.

Baal Shem Tov

The Troops of God

A true story

> "Let no man be held lightly in your eyes, for there is no man that does not have his time."
> – *Ethics of the Fathers* 4:3

Jerusalem is a city that can arouse strong emotions. But perhaps no emotion is stronger, or stranger, than a bizarre mental disorder known as "Jerusalem Syndrome." Jerusalem Syndrome can affect anyone, young or old, visitor or resident. It can strike within days of arriving in the Holy City and it may never abate. Jerusalem syndrome is known to affect people in one of three ways. Either (1) residents of Jerusalem become highly motivated – usually toward some positive, lofty and idealistic goal. A spirit of holiness enters into them, driving them relentlessly; (2) Jerusalem Syndrome may produce the opposite effect. Visitors to Jerusalem find it dark, foreboding, and depressing. A heavy air rests over the city, and they cannot wait to leave. This reaction is usually experienced by the more care-free, beach-loving, Tel Aviv crowd, or (3) Jerusalem makes some people crazy.

But here we must draw a distinction. The type of craziness that Jerusalem engenders is not like the madness found in other world metropolises. Eccentricity would be a better description for it, or perhaps it is some remnant of prophecy. The Talmud states, "From the day the Holy Temple was destroyed, prophecy was taken from the prophets and given to madmen and children." The Wall Street Journal of December 30, 1991, carried the following article: "Jerusalem Syndrome Makes Some Visitors Believe They're God: Israeli Doctors Are Puzzled by the Temporary Illness – They come as tourists, hoping to sightsee and relax. But they end up shouting prophecies from street corners, walking around naked and proclaiming themselves the Messiah."

If you consider for a moment, you will realize that all three forms of Jerusalem Syndrome are actually different manifestations of the same phenomena. In Jerusalem there is an abundance of spiritual light – it can either lift one up, or cast one down. The only difference lies in the vessels each person brings to receive it, and for some, their vessels are simply not strong enough. This explains why certain neighborhoods seem to have a higher incidence of Jerusalem Syndrome victims; for the closer one approaches holiness, the more intense the light becomes, and the more unusual is the behavior one is likely to encounter. The Old City and the Western Wall are among these places.

This is a story about Shmuel (not his real name), whose home is the Kotel. There he sleeps, there he eats, there he prays and there he sings to God. Whatever his past may have been, whoever he was before coming to Jerusalem, is unimportant. Since then, his life has become one great dedication of song, prayer and the Western Wall. He is a short, chubby, Sephardic man, perhaps in his late fifties. His long white beard and unkempt *peyos* offset his ruddy cheeks. He

The Troops of God

has dreamy, half closed eyes and a warm smile. Above all, Shmuel is best known for his generous voice. One always knows when he is approaching the Kotel, for his singing fills the courtyard. "The Moshiach is coming, the Moshiach is coming," he sings. And when the children mock him by shouting, "He's not coming, he's not coming" he sings back, unperturbed, "Oh, yes he is! Oh yes he is!" When he prays, everyone knows it. His *"Borchu et Adonai hamevorach,"* and *"Y'hei Shmei Rabbah..."* are always recited at the top of his lungs, and echo through the courtyard into everyone else's awareness.

Somehow, he has acquired a set of keys to the innermost, underground passageways of the Kotel, and late at night his voice can be heard singing Psalms from the depths of the catacombs. One morning he came skipping out of some hidden chamber, joyfully scattering coins at all the people praying. Another time, he showed up waving two, brightly lit sparklers. Tisha b'Av night, he stands by the Kotel loudly reciting Psalms until dawn, much to the consternation of the many who are trying to sleep a little during the traditional all-night vigil. On a recent Israeli television program about the Western Wall, his picture was featured with the caption, "Shmuel, the Man of the Kotel" - a title awarded to relatively few individuals in Jewish history.

So now, our story begins. It was a beautiful, cool night in early autumn. A half-moon shone brightly over the Old City walls. Scattered clouds floated lightly in the breeze. The Kotel was quiet. Here and there a few men stood in silent prayer. By one of the tables, a number of chasidim engaged in hushed conversation, waiting for the next evening prayer service to begin. It was a time of prayer and quiet introspection.

Then, suddenly, from up by the parking lot, about one

hundred yards away, a loud noise was heard, the sound of many voices, and running feet. All at once, from out of the darkness, about seventy-five young men, Israeli soldiers, ran into the Kotel courtyard. Tall, young, suntanned, with grey-green uniforms, high lace-up boots, and floppy, desert hats. Where had they come from? Where were they going? No one knows. Perhaps it was their night off for a bit of Jerusalem site-seeing. Perhaps they were part of a convoy moving from one base to another, and decided to spend a few moments at this holy spot along the way. How many were noticeably religious? A few knitted *kippot* stuck out from beneath the hats here and there, but for the most part, these soldiers seemed to have directed their lives in areas beyond the strictly sacred. With a great rushing sound, they filled the Kotel courtyard. Side by side, they fell into a long line against the length of the Wall. Each man rested his head upon his upraised arm, lost in his own thoughts or prayers – if he knew how to pray. They stood there for a long moment, quiet… waiting.

And then, in the clear, cool Jerusalem night, a familiar voice rang out through the courtyard and echoed off the stones. "SHEMA…" the voice cried out, and in perfect unison, like one man, the seventy-five soldiers responded "SHEMA!"

"YISRAEL," the voice continued.

"YISRAEL!" they all shouted.

"ADONAI ELOHEINU, ADONAI ECHAD."

There, standing behind the soldiers and shouting out commands like a seasoned drill sergeant, to everyone's amazement, was Shmuel, the Man of the Kotel. He continued: "*V'ahavta et Adonai Elohecha b'chol l'vav'cha uv'chol nafsh'cha uv'chol me'odecha.*" And after every single word, the entire battalion responded in unison. Like the well-trained fighting unit they were, they echoed his every word, his every intonation. No one interrupted, no one stepped out of line, no one paused to ask, "What do you think you are doing?" These men were soldiers – they knew how to take orders. And this man was a general – he knew how to give them.

Word by word they repeated after him, as he slowly recited the entire first paragraph of the *Shema*. When he reached the end, *"uch'sav'tam al mezuzot beitecha u'v'she'arecha,"* surely, onlookers thought, he would stop. One paragraph was enough for these impatient young men. He couldn't expect them to recite *all* of *Krias Shema*. But no, Shmuel kept on going, and they kept on repeating. *"V'hay'ah im shomo'a tishm'u et mitzvotai"* Again, they faithfully repeated single every word. Not that they had any choice. From the sound of Shmuel's voice, it was clear that anyone stepping out of line would be court-marshalled on the spot. Slowly Shmuel recited the entire *Krias Shema*. At his discretion, he repeated certain words in order to highlight them to the soldiers.

"Daber el B'nei Yisrael."

"Yisrael," the soldiers repeated.

"Yisrael!"

"Yisrael," they shouted back.

"YISRAEL!"

"L'maan tizk'ru v'asitem et kol mitzvotai, v'h'yitem kedoshim!"*

"Kedoshim!"

"KEDOSHIM!"

The dozen or so bystanders, who moments before had been idly waiting around, now stood in utter amazement.

---

* So that you shall remember and perform all My commandments and be holy (*kedoshim*) to your God. (Numbers 15:40).

Then, slowly, a spirit entered them as well. A spirit of unity, of humility, and of respect. They, too, stepped up to the Kotel and joined the soldiers in their prayer. A chasid, a yeshivah *bachur*, a *ba'al teshuvah* – all enlisted themselves in the troops of God.

After what seemed to be a very long time, Shmuel finally reached the end of *Krias Shema*. "*Ani Adonai Eloheichem... EMET.*" "*EMET!*" the soldiers all shouted – "TRUTH!" And with that last beautiful word, they turned from the Kotel, and with their steps full of autumn breeze, ran out of the courtyard back to their waiting transport. Shmuel ran along with them a ways, singing "*David, Melech Yisrael, Chai, Chai, v'Kayam...*" and they sang with him as they ran. A moment later they were gone, whisked off to their next destination, leaving the Kotel silent once again. Shmuel came trotting back to continue his usual form of worship. A number of young men went up to him and shook his hand. "*Mazel tov*, Shmuel, *mazel tov! Zachita!* You were meritorious!" But he was unimpressed. His eyes had already returned to their half-closed, dreamy gaze. He smiled a little, and then, taking a book of Psalms in hand, went back to his beloved Kotel to continue his prayers.

The Troops of God

The Torah compares Israel to the dust of the earth, the stars of the heavens, and the sand of the sea. This is to show the greatness of the Jewish people. For a plot of earth is a single unit, whereas the stars of heaven are unique and alone, while sand exhibits both traits: it forms a single stretch of land, yet each grain is unique.

Likewise, the Jewish people are one and united, yet each individual is as special and unique as a star in the sky.

R. Moshe Yechiel HaLevi of Ozharov
Be'er Moshe, Devorim 1:11

God takes a unique pride in each and every Jew – even the lowest one, even Jewish sinners. As long as he is still identified as a "Jew" (being called a "Jewish" sinner), God takes special pride in him, too. This is true down to the smallest detail. Sometimes, some base Jew merely shakes his sidelock, and God takes immense pride in this, as well.

R. Nachman of Breslov
Likutey Moharan 1:17

THE HEART

*Above all else, guard your heart,
for from it flow the springs of life.*

– Proverbs 4:23

SEVERAL YEARS AGO, I WAS INVITED TO A meeting with a leading spiritual teacher from another tradition (Thubten Chodron). It was an interesting dialogue, and we found that we had a lot in common – both of us were Jewish, both started pursuing spirituality at around the same age, both rejected our middle-class upbringings. At the end of the meeting, we brought the discussion down to brass tacks.

"So, what has twenty years of spiritual practice brought you?"

"I think that it's opened my heart a little," was the answer we both gave.

A worthwhile payoff for a twenty year investment, I still believe.

Solomon's Dream

The heart is the king of the body
— *Tikuney Zohar*

The king is the heart of the nation
— *Maimonides*

So many hearts beat in this world – wise hearts and broken hearts, stone hearts, and hearts of flesh. "A pure heart create in me, O Lord, and an upright spirit renew within me" (Psalms 51:12). And so rich is the life of a single heart, as the Midrash says: "The heart sees, the heart hears, the heart speaks, the heart walks, the heart falls, the heart rejoices, the heart cries out, the heart comforts, the heart suffers, the heart surrenders, the heart errs, the heart trembles, the heart awakens…"

Of all the hearts that are in this world, of all the riches that a person could ever long for, I am always so moved by the story of King Solomon, and the heart that he requested from God:

> In Givon, the Lord appeared to Solomon in a dream by night. And God said, Ask what I shall grant you. And Solomon said, You have shown great faithful love to Your servant David, my father, because he walked before

> You in faithfulness and righteousness and in integrity of heart. And You have kept for him this great faithful love, by giving him a son to sit on his throne, as it is this day. And now, O Lord, my God, You have made Your servant king in place of my father David, yet I am but a lad... Give, then, Your servant a listening heart to judge Your people, to distinguish between good and evil; for who can judge this vast people of Yours?" (1 Kings 3:5-9)

King Solomon could have asked for anything, and received it; yet he longed for a "listening heart." It is not merely that he understood this to be the most important thing in the world; he realized that this is the very essence of *all* things in the world, bearing the power to draw all things toward it. For one who has this can have everything, as we see from the verses that follow:

> And God was pleased that Solomon had asked for this. And God said to him, Because you have asked for this thing, and did not ask for long life, nor have you asked for riches, nor have you asked for the life of your enemies, but have asked for discernment to listen in judgment, behold, I have done as you have spoken. I have given you a heart that is wise and understanding; so that there has never been anyone like you before, nor shall anyone like you arise again. And I will also give you that which you have not asked for, both riches and glory all your life, the like of which no king has ever had (Ibid. 10-13).

Solomon asked for a listening heart, and in receiving it, received everything else as well. The heart has the power to draw to itself all things in the world, because the heart is the place of all things in the world; it provides the context in which everything finds meaning. Rabbi Nachman of Breslov said: "For a person with heart, you cannot speak of 'place.' The opposite is true; he is the place of the world. Because God is the 'place' of the world, and Godliness is in the heart. Therefore, a person with a heart should never say, 'this place is not good,' for he does not truly exist in place. He Himself is the place of the entire world."

A listening heart is always open, sensitive to the joy and pain of others, offering a space within itself for the other to enter. It gives each person what he so badly needs – an affirmation of his place in this world. But not just any place. In Kabbalah, the wisdom of the heart is called *Binah* (as opposed to *Chochmah*, the wisdom of the head). *Binah* is related to the word *Boneh*, "to build," for the heart's wisdom is always constructive, seeking to build, to set a person on his feet, to put him in his place. It listens beneath the surface of a person's words, and hears, within all his struggles and searching, the essence of desire – which is the longing to find that place where a person can grow in love.

> And Solomon awoke; and behold, it was a dream. And he went to Jerusalem and stood before the Ark of the Covenant of the Lord, and offered up burnt offerings and peace offerings, and made a feast for all his servants.
>
> Then two women who were prostitutes came before the King. And one woman said, O my lord, this woman and I live in the same house, and I gave birth to a child while she was in the house. And it came to pass on the third day after I delivered, that this woman also gave birth to a child. We were alone; there was no one else with us in the house, just the two of us. And this woman's child died in the night, because she lay on it. And

she arose in the night, and took my son from beside me while your maidservant slept, and laid him in her bosom; and she laid her dead son in my bosom. When I awoke in the morning to nurse my child, he was dead; but when I looked at him closely in the morning, it was not the son that I had borne.

Then the other woman said, No; for the live child is my son, and the dead one is yours. But the first one insisted, No, the dead boy is yours, the live one is mine! And they went on arguing before the king.

Then the king said, One says, this is my son, and the dead one is yours, and the other says, No, the dead boy is yours, mine is the live one. So the king said, Bring me a sword. And they brought a sword before the king. And the king said, Cut the live child in two, and give half to one and half to the other.

But the woman whose son was the live one pleaded with the king, for she was overcome with love for her son. Please, my lord, she cried, give her the live child, only do not kill it. But the other insisted, It shall be neither yours nor mine, cut it in two. Then the king spoke up and said, Give her the live child, and do not kill it, for she is its mother (Ibid. 3:27).

Solomon did not judge with his mind. He did not seek out witnesses, nor interrogate the two women. He listened with his heart until he could discern the true mother's voice, which was the voice of love – the only voice that the heart truly recognizes. By doing so, he returned the child to its place. For had the wrong mother raised it, the child would have been far from its place, and never received the love that it needed to grow.

The Talmud says that all kingship on earth is a reflection of the Kingship in Heaven. If so, then God must have a listening heart, as well.

According to the Kabbalah, God created the world in order to make known His attribute of Kingship, as the Sages said, "There is no king without a people." However, in order to do this, He had to make a space in His infinite Being where creation could exist. In other words, before He created the world, He had to make a place for the world. "When it arose in the simple Divine will to emanate a creation... God withdrew Himself to the sides, in the center of His light, leaving an empty space. In this space, exist all the worlds." God created the universe at the center of His infinite Being – that is, in His very heart. There it is nurtured, and there it grows. This is the esoteric meaning of the verse, "My heart is empty within me" (Psalms 109:22). Once the heart is emptied, it can become a place for all creation.

It was with this heart that King Solomon judged the people of Israel, for judgment depends upon the heart, as the verse says: "And Aharon shall carry the judgment of the children of Israel upon his heart" (Exodus 28:30). The essence of judgment lies in facing a situation in which things are askew, and restoring each element to its rightful place, where it can once again flourish. The heart alone can accomplish this – not simply because it knows the place of everything in the world, but because it *is* the place of everything in the world. The heart knows where everything belongs, because ultimately, everything belongs within it.

> And God gave Solomon wisdom and great understanding, and a heart as broad as the sand upon the seashore.... And he spoke of the trees, from the cedar tree in Lebanon,

to the hyssop that grows out of the wall, and he spoke of the beasts, and the birds, and the creeping things, and the fishes (Ibid. 5:9-14).

A person with a listening heart yearns constantly to hear where all things belong. He seeks to return all things to their proper place, where they can grow with love - the birds, the beasts, even the fatherless son of a lonely prostitute. He listens in judgment, which, ultimately, is part of the very movement of humanity toward redemption: the return to God's kingdom, and the return to our hearts - to that time when everything will find its place.

Thus says the Lord, the God of Israel: Like these good figs, so shall I show favor upon those that are carried away captive of Judah, whom I have driven out of this place to the land of the Chaldeans. I will set my eyes upon them for the good, and I will bring them again to this land; I will build them, and not pull them down; I will plant them, and not pluck them up. And I will give them a heart to know Me, that I am the Lord. And they shall be My people, and I will be their God, for they shall return to Me with all their heart (Jeremiah 24:5-7).

A Change of Clothing

Evening had fallen. Rabbi Shmuel Schneersohn, the fourth Lubavitcher Rebbe, sat in his private study and counseled his chasidim. One by one they entered, young and old, rich and poor, broken of spirit or content. Each one poured out his heart to his Rebbe. They begged him for his advice and blessings, for health, livelihood, and success in serving God. Reb Shmuel listened to each one intently, answering him with wisdom and compassion. After about an hour, however, he was exhausted. He took a break, and called for a change of clothing. As the attendant carried away the old clothes, he noticed that they were drenched with sweat. He was amazed. Was there something wrong with the Rebbe? Reb Shmuel noticed his inquiring expression.

"You're wondering why they are so wet? Well, I'll explain. All of these people turn to me for advice. But in order for me to help them, I must feel their problems as if they were my own. I must put aside my own perspective and clothe myself in theirs – their pain, their trouble, and their joy. But then, in order to help them, I have to return to who I am, for otherwise, why would they be coming to me?

"Have you ever tried changing your clothes forty times in one hour? Can you imagine how exhausted you would be? Well, changing your entire personality – all of your feelings and intellect – is infinitely harder."

❧ RELATIONSHIPS ☙

*So God created man in His own image,
in the image of God He created him;
male and female He created them.*

– Genesis 1:27

I MARRIED RATHER LATE IN LIFE, AT LEAST, for an Orthodox Jew – a month before turning thirty-eight. And this was after ten years of intensive dating. There is much to learn to make a successful marriage, and – especially for late starters – much to unlearn.

I wrote the first draft of this article in the weeks before my wedding, for a *Parabola* issue on the topic of "Conscience and Consciousness." Due to the wedding preparations, I was not able to complete it at that time, and only finished it years later, when an issue was being planned on the theme of "Marriage."

Twenty years and five children later, I find my insights to still be correct.

Standing Beneath the Mountain

It is three days before my wedding and everything is ready, the hall, the band, the catering. Only one thing is not ready... I am not ready. It is not merely that I feel overwhelmed by the myriads of untried responsibilities that await me, nor do I mourn the inevitable loss of freedom that married life brings. The reason is much simpler – I barely know my bride-to-be.

Despite its almost unquestioned espousal in the Western world, the contemporary approach to wedlock is by no means universal. Many traditional societies still practice some form of arranged marriage. The Chasidic community, with which I have been associated for over a decade, continues to subscribe to this model. Although "Fiddler on the Roof" style engagements are a thing of the past, romance is definitely not a factor in the decision-making process. Rather, the procedure is as follows: Matchmakers are called in, parents thoroughly research their prospective son or daughter-in-law and their families. If things look promising, the couple meets – but only once or twice. (I met a full six times before proposing!) If both partners agree, they will not see each other again until the wedding night. And there is *never* any form of pre-marital physical contact.

Were you to ask the couple why they are marrying, they

would probably respond: "Because it says so in the Torah!" Actually, what it says is: "Be fruitful and multiply" (Genesis 1:28), which the Rabbis interpreted as the obligation to marry and raise a family. By the time the wedding night arrives, the bride and groom in an "arranged" marriage are no less excited than any others – probably they are more so. However, after the initial excitement wanes, the couple will find that their relationship is built upon foundations more solid than most – principles that transcend the ego and its concerns. For while love ebbs and flows, if a marriage is to last, it must be tied to something more enduring than personal feelings.

Approached this way, marriage becomes one of the primary tools for spiritual growth and for developing the qualities of commitment and responsibility. One must learn to care for one's spouse despite their moods, their attractiveness (or occasional lack of it), and even when they do not fulfill one's expectations. Marrying "because it says so" places the rationale for this most challenging relationship outside of oneself, and the transcendence of self is the necessary prerequisite for any successful marriage.

This approach is not limited to matrimony; it is a way of relating to all of life. The Hebrew word that best captures it is *tzedek*. While often translated as "justice" or "righteousness," *tzedek* means dealing with the world in terms of its objective needs, not according to personal benefits. Thus *tzedakah*, usually translated as "charity," really means helping the poor because it is the right thing to do, because their condition demands our help. And a Tzaddik – an enlightened individual – is one so fully attuned to the needs of others and of situations around him that his care for them transcends his own personal concerns.

This idea reflects one of the most important aspects of Jewish spirituality – the union of law and revelation.

When the Jewish people stood at Mount Sinai, they experienced a direct encounter with the Divine. "Only take heed and watch yourself very carefully, lest you forget the things that your eyes saw... the day you stood before the Lord your God at Horeb... You drew near and stood under the mountain; and the mountain burned with fire unto the heart of heaven, with darkness, cloud and mist. Then God spoke to you out of the fire..." (Deuteronomy 4:9-11). It was a moment of purified consciousness, of unity with the Infinite. Yet, at that same instant, God delivered the Ten Commandments, the moral basis of society: "You heard the voice of words, but saw no image; there was only a voice. He declared to you His covenant, instructing you to keep the Ten Commandments, and He wrote them on two tablets of stone" (ibid 4:12-13). The fact that these events occurred simultaneously suggests that they are not separate in nature, but two aspects of a single phenomenon.

The message of Mount Sinai is that there is an intrinsic connection between higher consciousness and ethical behavior. Enlightenment is not neutral, for the mind freed of the self is naturally drawn to actions that heal and repair the world. Judaism has always made this connection. Throughout Jewish history, there has been little dichotomy between the esoteric and exoteric practice of the tradition, and many of the great mystics were also great legal scholars. The Midrash goes as far as stating that the Patriarchs – Abraham, Isaac, and Jacob – observed all the laws of the Torah long before it was given, as a consequence of their spiritual attachment to God. This implies that true enlightenment is not a matter of transcending morality, but of embodying it, and it suggests a unity of consciousness and conscience.

When the Israelites stood at Sinai, states the Talmud, they were reluctant to accept the Torah – not until God uprooted the mountain and held it over their heads: "If you accept My Torah, fine," He declared. "If not, this mountain will be your burial place." Chasidic texts explain this as a metaphor for the intensity of the revelation. The Presence of God weighed down upon them so overwhelmingly that is was irrefusable. "The Torah was given by force, and it is transmitted by force," said the Komarno Rebbe. So too, moments of consciousness – whether of higher consciousness or simple moments of clarity – should be reflected in ethical behavior, in the voice of conscience that prompts one to act beyond the values of the self. Thus, an enlightened person is not only fully conscious, but "fully conscience" – the embodiment of conscience. For the two are one: inner revelation finds expression in outer actions, and ethical behavior can lead one to inner illumination.

And this is the essence of marriage. It is the day-to-day practice of enlightenment. For instance, if I return home one night to find that my young wife has burned the chicken dinner, spilled the soup on the floor, and broken the oven door (though I hope she will not), and I become angry with her and turn my face away (though I hope I will not), it is a sign that I am no longer in a conscious relationship with the situation, and all the more so, with my wife. My own self-interests have obscured me to the truth of a situation that demands my care and attention. Thousands of such scenarios are possible. However, while consciousness may leave a person, conscience rarely does. It hangs over one's head like a mountain, pressing upon a person to make amends, and to return to a conscious relationship with one's spouse and with life.

Ultimately, our conscience is what weds us to the present moment. For to truly live in this world, one must be married to the world. To love the world because it is the face of God, to give to it and be aware of its needs. Not to become angry when it fails one's expectations, nor upset when it contradicts one's will, but to tend to each situation with love and attention, with justice and compassion, for it holds the presence of God. "The purely righteous do not complain about evil," said the great mystic, Rabbi Abraham Isaac Kook, "rather they add justice. They do not complain about heresy, rather they add faith. They do not complain about ignorance, rather they add wisdom." Such a person hears the echo of Sinai in every moment of life.

How then, does one begin married life with a stranger? It requires adjustment, concession, and the endless ability to forgive. And it demands gratuitous love, constant giving, and the relinquishing of expectations. Let's not forget that the Chasidic community is a closely-knit, highly supportive society. Young people come to their wedding night with many shared values. In addition, a healthy sex-life, encouraged by the Torah, goes a long way to building emotional closeness. Judaism does not have a monastic tradition, but stresses marriage and family life as a path to holiness.

Nevertheless, there is no avoiding the inner work, which is, in fact, the same work that every couple must do if their marriage is to succeed. It has been said that no one ever marries a real person – people marry their illusions. Real marriage begins when the illusions fade and one comes face-to-face with one's spouse. "Face to face, God spoke with you at the mountain, from out of the fire" (Deuteronomy 5:4).

It means crossing that fine line between what I want and what God wants for me. In an arranged marriage, one does not say, "I married my spouse because I love him"; rather, "I love him because I married him." This is less difficult than it sounds; it is how we all have children. No one says, "I loved my children, therefore I had them" – it works the other way around. When you can be fully present to someone, you will come to love them.

Kabbalah teaches that every human relationship is a metaphor for the relationship between man and God. This is certainly true of marriage. The Midrash says that at Sinai, a wedding ceremony was held between the Jewish people and God. The Torah was the marriage contract, ministering angels served as bridesmaids, and the mountain itself was suspended over their heads like a wedding canopy. Because this is the essence of marriage – to live under the mountain. To be fully present to another. The Talmud says: "If a husband and wife are worthy, the Divine Presence dwells between them." For every marriage is a replay of Sinai, a covenant as binding as that between God and man.

> And it shall be on that day, says the Lord, that you shall call Me my Husband, and shall call Me no more my Master.... On that day, I will make a covenant for them with the beasts of the field, the birds of heaven, and the creeping things of the ground; and I will break the bow and the sword and the war out of the land, and will make them lie down safely.
>
> And I will betroth you to Me forever; I will betroth you to Me in righteousness and in justice, in love and in compassion. And I will betroth you to Me in faithfulness, and you shall know the Lord. (Hosea 2:18–22)

The Essence of Study

Late one night, Rabbi Dov Ber – the "Mitler Rebbe" of Chabad – was awake studying Torah in his parents' house in Liadi. Suddenly, there was a knock on his chamber door, and his father, Rabbi Shneur Zalman, the first Rebbe of Chabad, walked in. R. Dov Ber stood up in respect.

"My son, what were you studying just now?"

"I was studying the kabbalistic writings of the Arizal, father," R. Dov Ber replied.

"Do you find them profound?" R. Shneur Zalman asked.

"Father, they contain the secrets of the universe."

"And do they uplift you?"

"When I study them, I feel as if I were standing before the Divine Presence."

His father paused. "My son, several minutes ago, on the floor just below you, an infant fell out of a bed and was crying. I was upstairs, also studying. But when I heard it cry, I ran downstairs to help, for I assumed that you were asleep. We should never forget that no matter how profound and uplifting the study of Torah may be, one must never become so engaged that he fails to hear the cries of another human being.

Slim

A true story

Highway Seventeen stretches north from Phoenix to the Grand Canyon. I was traveling south, staring through the window of a Greyhound bus at the endless desert beyond. That's how I felt inside too, dry and dead. I had come to Arizona on a mission – to save a Jewish soul – but I had failed. Now I was returning home empty-handed, and my heart was broken.

After college, I spent some time on an Israeli kibbutz. There I met Rachel, a nice girl from Chicago, from the very neighborhood I had grown up in. I didn't know it at the time, but we were meeting at the crossroads. I was coming into Judaism after a secular upbringing, and she was falling away after a religious one. We were friends for a while. When I went back to the States I was surprised to discover that her family was Orthodox. In fact, her father was a rabbi who had written several books. It was in their house that I experienced my first Shabbos.

Rachel came back to Chicago, but she couldn't bear living with her family. She would visit me at my apartment sometimes, and we would talk. But eventually, she left town. She hooked up with some real lowlifes and moved down to

Slim

Arizona, to a small town near the Grand Canyon. She was with a bunch of weird guys living in a few broken-down trailers doing all sorts of strange stuff. When her parents found out about it, they were upset, of course. Rabbi Praeger, her father, called me up one day.

"Chaim, I know you were good friends with Rachel. We're asking you for a favor. Fly down to Arizona – we'll pay for the ticket – and speak to her. We're not asking for miracles. Just tell her we love her and we wish she would come home."

Well, you know, *ahavas Yisroel* is a great *mitzvah*, so I agreed. I flew to Phoenix and then took a bus north. When I got to the town, I called her up from a local phone. "Hi, Rachel, this is Chaim. How are you? I'm just passing through and I thought I would give you a call."

"Chaim! You're in town? I don't believe it!" We got together and talked, but I could tell right away that she wasn't leaving. I stayed in a trailer with a bunch of guys for several days; they were living in filth. Nothing I could say to Rachel made any difference.

"Chaim, I'm not going home. I'll leave here when I want to. It's nobody's business what I do." After three days, I couldn't take it anymore. I called Rabbi Praeger and told him the story. Then I left.

I took the first bus back to Phoenix. I felt sick. Here was someone I knew, someone I cared about; to see her in the dumps like that, in the lowest place, broke my heart.

It was about a three-hour ride to Phoenix. We drove across the Arizona desert, passed cowboy ranches, Indian reservations. It's still the Wild West down there. The bus continued on for forty minutes before pulling into a small town, St. John's, Arizona. A town? There were four stores: a hardware store, a feed store, a bar and a gas station. The bus wasn't even picking anyone up, just making a mail stop. Now, here comes my first wrong move. I was feeling all burnt-out inside; my stomach was still churning from the experience. I needed a beer, something to relax me, to pull me back together. So I told the bus driver I was getting off.

"Are you sure?" he asked. He looked at me like I was crazy. I was already wearing a *kippah* then, and my beard was even longer than today.

"Yeah," I said, "I'm sure." I unloaded my bags, and in a minute, I was standing on the asphalt watching the bus pulled away. I figured I would catch the next bus out a few hours later. It was noon, the sun was hot, the air was dry, nothing around for miles – just an empty highway and those few stores. I turned towards the bar. The blinds were drawn. As I put my hand on the doorknob, a thought crossed my mind: "Don't go in here." But it was too late, I opened the door and went in.

It was as if I had entered a motion picture. The place was full of cowboys, real ones, the ones that eat lead. The lights were dim; Merle Haggard music was playing in the background. Several men were shooting a game of pool and a few were playing poker in the corner. There was sawdust on the floor and a big mirror behind the bar with the words "Lone Star Beer" embossed on it. A long crack, like an ugly scar, stretched across its length.

I walked in and everything stopped. All eyes were upon me. The place was silent. I felt like Clint Eastwood. I walked up to the bar and sat on a stool. The bartender came over to me. He was a middle aged man, with a square face and closely cropped white hair. He had steel blue eyes and looked at me without blinking. He reminded me of an ex-marine sergeant.

Slim

"Boy, where you from?" He spoke quietly, with a thick southern accent.

"I'm from Chicago."

"What do you want?"

"I want a beer."

"How did you get here, boy?"

"I got off the bus that just came through."

"You got off the bus?" he paused. "Not many people get off the bus here... and nobody gets back on." He kept staring at me. I felt my heart starting to race. He was trying to frighten me, and was doing a good job. If you want to terrorize someone, speak in a whisper. The whole room was quiet, yet no one could hear him but me.

"We don't get many of your kind around here, boy."

"Well, I'm just passing through on my way to Phoenix. I hope to get on the next bus."

"There ain't no next bus till tomorrow, boy. That's a long time." He turned and walked away. He came back with a bottle of beer and banged it on the counter in front of me. I jumped at the sound.

"Where you gonna sleep, boy?"

"I guess I'll stay in a hotel."

"There ain't no hotels here, boy."

"Well, I've got a sleeping bag. I'll just put it out back somewhere."

"There are plenty of snakes and scorpions round these parts. A man could die out there." He gave a slight smirk. "We're gonna have a good old time tonight, boy," he said as he walked away. The cowboys all gathered around him and I could hear him relating my story... Chicago... Phoenix... passing through....

One of the cowboys heard I was from Chicago.

"CHICAGO!" he yelled. He came over and slapped me on the back. "I was in the navy in Chicago, boy. It's the best damn town in the world! I had more fun in Chicago than you could imagine!" So, for the next three hours this cowboy told me all the fun he had in Chicago – adventures that are not to be repeated. Meanwhile, I felt trapped. I had no place to go. I was scared to say anything. All these guys carried guns, at least two – a revolver on the waist and a shotgun besides their chair. So I listened and listened until the navy man finished talking and left me alone. In the meantime, I was getting a little dizzy from all the beers I had drunk. The music had picked up again, as had the card game and the billiards. Everything in the room started taking on heightened tones. But no one else spoke to me. It was as if I didn't exist. Around 7:30 at night the cowboy came up to me again.

"Boy, we ain't got no hotel here, like in Chicago. Don't you go sleepin' outside. You come back to my house. There's only me and my wife, all the kids have moved away. We've got plenty of room. You'll get a good night's rest. Tomorrow, when the bus comes in, we'll put you right back on, and off you go."

When another one of the cowboys heard that, he came up to me too.

"Boy," he said. "Don't listen to that fool. You like horses? I've got me the biggest horse ranch in all Arizona. You come back with me. Tomorrow morning we'll get up early and go ridin'. A man don't feel like a man 'til he's been on a horse."

"Well, thanks," I said. "I really appreciate that." I was trying to figure out what to do. Suddenly I felt a tap on my back. I turned around – and my breath stopped. There stood a man, in his early fifties, tall, stick thin, his entire face tracked with scars. Part of his right ear was missing. He had only a few chipped teeth in his mouth, and a four-day old beard. His forearms were covered with tatoos. He was wearing a torn denim shirt and torn jeans. A battered cowboy hat was pulled low over his forehead. He looked me straight in the eyes.

"Boy, my name is Slim." His voice was deep and rough. "I clean up this place. I know you got no place to stay. I got me a tent right out back. If you want, you can be my guest. I'll finish cleanin' up here and we can go out back." I was terrified. He looked like something out of an Alfred Hitchcock film, like a murderer.

Slim walked away and I took a deep breath. This was the last thing I needed. I looked around the bar for my other "friends." The fellow from Chicago came up to me.

"Did Slim just ask you to sleep with him tonight?" I nodded my head.

"Good," he said.

"Why?" I asked.

"You'll see." He walked away. The cowboy with the horse ranch also retreated from his offer. They were leaving me no alternatives. I went back up to Slim.

"I think I'll take you up on your offer, Slim," I stuttered.

"That's good," he said. "You've made me very happy." Slim went back to cleaning up, and I returned to my bar stool. At about 10:00 P.M. the bar closed down, and the rest of the cowboys went home. The bartender left and Slim locked the door behind him. He mopped the floor and washed the glasses. At about 10:30 he finished.

"All right, boy. You ready to go home?" He opened up the back door of the bar and showed me his small tent. There was enough room in it for the two of us. A little light filtered in from the bar, but most of the light came from the stars. I went inside and unrolled my sleeping bag.

"Boy," he said. "I know you're hungry. I've been watchin' you all day. You didn't eat a thing. Let me get you some bread and coffee." He went into the bar and made a pot of coffee. I had some peanut butter and made some sandwiches. The whole time I was eating, Slim just sat there on his mat, staring at me. He didn't blink, he didn't take his eyes off me. I was sure he was psychotic. I didn't know what to do with myself. I was getting more nervous by the moment.

"Boy, you ready to go to sleep now?" Slim asked when I finished eating.

"I guess so."

"Well, let's get to it."

What's next, I thought. What am I getting set up for? I climbed into my sleeping bag. Slim sat there staring at me. He had a pistol in his belt and a rifle on the floor. My heart was racing. "What's he going to do to me?" I thought. "There's going to be a fight, I know it. But I'm sure I can take him." I had played college football and was still pretty strong. "But even if I beat him up, where can I go? These cowboys will all come looking for me. I'm in the middle of the desert. Where can I run? They'll come after me on their damn horses. They'll find me, bring me back and kill me. Then they'll have a good laugh for a few weeks about that Jew-boy from Chicago they killed." I closed my eyes and pretended to be asleep. I snuck a look at Slim through my half-closed lids. He was still sitting there staring at me. I tried to calm myself down. I started counting my breaths. I couldn't fight if I was so tense. One… two… three… I started to calm down. I was ready for anything.

Suddenly, Slim made a move. I nearly jumped. My heart started racing again. Cold sweat broke out on my forehead. My fists were clenched hard.

Slim

Slim got up from his mat. But instead of coming towards me, he walked outside the tent. I watched him through the open door. His lean silhouette was framed against the stars. He stood there silently for a moment, then he raised his hands to the sky.

"Lord," he prayed. "Good Lord. I spent ten years in prison for killin' a man. I didn't mean to do it, but I killed him. And all those years I thought you hated me. But I had a lot of time then to read Your Bible and learn about Your children, and I know who they are. When a man trusts another man with his son, that shows there is love between them. I have one of your children here in my tent, and I'm watchin' over him. I have children too, but I don't know where they are. They all left me. Lord, I beg You. I'll watch over Your child, and You watch over mine."

I couldn't believe it. I started to cry. He didn't want to kill me. He was just waiting for me to go to sleep so he could go outside and pray to God.

"And Lord," Slim continued. "I want to thank You for what You have given me, and for all the blessings in my life. Thank You for my work. Thank You for my home. Thank You for bringing me one of Your children to watch over. And I hope that from this day on, You and I will come closer and closer together, because now I know that You love me and forgive me."

After a few more minutes of prayer, he came inside the tent, got into his sleeping bag and fell into a deep sleep.

The next morning, I woke up with renewed strength. Slim was already inside the bar setting things up. I put on my *tefillin* and prayed. I felt free, happy. No one could touch me. Slim came in and out. He knew I was praying and didn't interrupt. Afterwards, I went into the bar and he made me a cup of coffee. We didn't share many words, but there was a deep communion between us. At about 10:00 A.M., the cowboys started coming in, drinking coffee, hanging around. Sometime later, the cowboy from the navy came in. He walked right up to me and asked in a low voice, "Did Slim speak to God last night?"

"He did," I responded.

"He's been doin' that every night for twenty years," he said, and walked away.

At about 1:00 P.M. the bus pulled in. Everyone in the bar accompanied me out. Slim put my bags in the luggage compartment while I shook hands with the whole crowd. They all smiled and were friendly. When I reached the door of the bus, Slim was standing there waiting. He grabbed me and gave me a big hug. "Son," he said. "If you ever need me, you know where I am. Just give me a call and I'll be there for you." He gave me another hug and a kiss on the cheek. The bus driver – the same one from yesterday – stared at us in disbelief. I got on the bus and found a seat besides the window. They were all waving at me. "Bye, Chaim. Bye." They knew my name by then. "Come back soon!" Then off we went. I arrived in Phoenix and caught the next available flight to Chicago.

When I arrived home, I went to speak to Rabbi Praeger. I told him about his daughter, and about Slim. He was quiet for a long time. "Chaim," he said. "It was worth it."

Song of the Shepherds

It was Sabbath morning and the congregation was singing the songs of praise in the morning prayers. Rabbi Tzvi Elimelech of Dinov stepped over to the *shul's* broad-framed window. He gazed out over the valley below – over the rolling green hills, the fields rich with crops, the amber blue sky. And when his heart was filled with love and praise for the Creator, he sang the words of the *Nishmas* prayer:

> The soul of all living things shall praise Your Name, Lord our God, and the spirit of all flesh shall always glorify and exalt Your remembrance, our King… To You alone we give thanks. If our mouths were filled with song like the sea, and our tongues with joyous song like the roar of the waves, our lips with praise like the expanse of heaven, and our eyes were to shine like the sun and the moon. If our hands were spread out like the wings of the eagle, and our feet were as swift as the hinds, it would not be enough to thank you, Lord our God and God of our fathers, and to bless Your Name for even one of the thousands and myriads of favors, miracles and wonders that You have done for us and our fathers…

Every week he sung these words, while the congregation hummed quietly along in rapture. So beautiful was the melody that the gentile shepherds would gather their flocks in the valley beneath the *shul* to hear his song of praise.

But time went by. The Dinover Rebbe became old. He fell into ill health, and at last, left this world for higher realms. The week of his passing was hard for his congregation, but those moments in *shul* on Shabbos morning were the hardest of all. With heavy hearts the congregation sang the morning psalms, and a solemn air hung over the room as they approached those special verses of praise. Then, suddenly, just as they were about to intone the words of *Nishmas*, the familiar melody rose up from outside the *shul* and floated in through the window.

The congregation ran to the window in disbelief. There, below, the Gentile shepherds were singing the praises of God. They had gathered together as usual, and spontaneously, the Dinover Rebbe's wonderful song had broken forth from their lips.

Song of the Shepherds

God's main honor comes when individuals who were outside the bounds of holiness, such as converts or *baalei teshuvah*, bring themselves within. Then God's Name is glorified above and below. His honor ascends to its root, and peace is drawn into the world.

Thus, no person should ever think that his misdeeds have taken him so far from God that he cannot return; for the further away a person is, the more he glorifies God when he brings himself back. This is God's main honor.

R. NACHMAN OF BRESLOV
Likutey Moharan 1:14

"And Devorah, a prophetess... judged Israel at that time" – *Judges 4:4*

Why was Devorah a judge at that time, seeing that Pinchas, the son of Elazar (the son of Aharon HaKohen) was still alive?

On this, I call upon Heaven and earth to be my witnesses, that any person – Jew or non-Jew, man or woman, slave or maidservant – can attain *ruach hakodesh*; it only depends upon one's deeds.

Tanna d'Bei Eliyahu Rabbah 9

CHANGES

For every thing there is a season, and a time to every purpose under the heaven.

– Ecclesiastes 3:1

AS A PERSON CHANGES IN LIFE, SO DOES HIS or her relationship to the Torah. After college, I imagined I would be enlightened within the year. That did not prove to be the case. It's now thirty years later, and my goals are somewhat different (for better or for worse).

It's said that there are seventy faces to the Torah, that is, seventy different modes of interpretation. It also says: "The days of our years are seventy" (Psalms 90:10); for each year corresponds to a different approach to Torah. The main thing is that they should all be for the good, as the verse says about Abraham: "And Abraham was old; he came with his days" (Genesis 24:1). "He came with *all of* his days," adds the Zohar.

The Temple of Amount

It has been years since I've enjoyed the sweetness of a symbolic life, since the time when the world spoke to me like a metaphor. In those youthful days of spiritual awakening, the world was strangely transparent, and every chance encounter, every passing sight, held out the promise of deeper meaning. All of life pointed to the existence of a higher reality. It was a time of openness and wonder, and of deep contemplation.

And so I became religious, for religious life is symbolic life, devoted to uncovering the truths that lie beneath the surface of this world. Every symbol carries some inner meaning, whether simple or complex. In all cases, a symbol is an entity whose content is greater than its form, for with just a few lines or gestures, it conveys a message that would otherwise require many words. But precisely because of this meager form, because their meaning is not overt, symbols demand that the viewer reconstruct the original message *within himself*. As such, they are vehicles for inner transformation, and are among the primary tools of the religious life, which seeks to convey truths that are altogether beyond words. Symbols are points of contemplation, for only by dwelling upon them, do they reveal their contents. And the more one contemplates them, the more meaningful they become. Furthermore, religious symbols, whose subject is the Infinite, have the potential to convey infinite meaning.

In Judaism, symbols give expression to every facet and stage of life: symbols of covenant, of renewal, of redemption – from the bitter herb eaten Passover night, symbolizing the harshness of exile, to the blast of the shofar on the New Year, symbolizing the great horn of Messiah. The Torah puts such emphasis on symbols because it understands that, ultimately, all of life is symbolic, and that the entire creation is only a vehicle through which we relate to God. Torah study is above all an exercise in interpretation. Texts are endlessly examined for their inner meaning, and new interpretations are put forth constantly. For by learning to uncover the inner meaning of a text, one can eventually learn to uncover the inner meaning of the world. And when the world is understood as a symbol in the Divine-human relationship, then its every detail is also seen to contain the potential for infinite meaning.

Yet, while all things can be meditated upon to discover God's presence, ultimately, the most important symbol is the human form itself, which reflects the Divine Image. "From my very flesh, I will behold God," says the prophet (Job 19:26). According to Kabbalah, contemplation upon the different aspects of the human dimension – one's thoughts, feelings and actions – can lead a person to an understanding of the Divine attributes. For the human arm is only a symbol of God's "arm" – His power and influence in the world. The human heart is only a reflection of the Divine heart; yet through it, we can learn about His infinite love for creation.

Within the human dimension, the richest symbol of all is the self, and contemplating the self is the primary means of apprehending something of the Divine Being. The beauty of contemplative life is that it allows a person time to engage in a pure act of self-reflection, until the self yields up its secret as the very expression of God's Being – His *malchus* – in the world. Through contemplation upon the "I" of the self, one can achieve knowledge of the true "I" of creation. On the verse, "I am Pharaoh" (Genesis 41:44), the Midrash comments: "From the 'I am' of flesh and blood, one can deduce the "I AM" of the Holy One." Even the "I am" of Pharaoh – the Biblical paradigm of selfishness and egotism – can eventually bring a person to the realization of the true "I AM" of creation.

However, all that was years ago. Today I am lost in a world of numbers. The great challenge of a life devoted to symbols is the constant need to penetrate ever deeper into their hidden meaning. No symbol remains relevant forever. After a time, the personal meaning found in the symbol begins to lessen: words of prayer become empty, religious images become hollow. What is called for now is a new act of contemplation, a further opening of the mind and heart to God. But at this important juncture, there lies the possibility of a mistake, that a person will look elsewhere for fulfillment. To do so is to leave the world of symbols and enter the realm of numbers, where quantity, rather than depth, serves as the criteria for meaning. It is not a question of how many symbols a person has at the center of his life, but in which direction he turns when the meaningful elements of life fall silent. This can be thought of in terms of a relationship. What do you do when the relationship with a loved one fails? Do you look elsewhere for love, or do you look deeper? Eventually, the new symbol will also lose its meaning, as will all those that follow. But once this horizontal movement has been established – this constant pursuit of the novel – one soon forgets the intrinsic value of things, and judges them solely in relative, external terms. Worth becomes a product of amount, of "how much," and "how many."

I do not remember when I fell away from the symbolic life – it must have happened gradually – but I am aware of the consequences. It is the difference between feeling fulfilled in life and feeling empty, between a sense of closeness to God, and the fear that one is never doing enough. On the lowest level, it manifests itself in the pursuit of meaning through material acquisition. On the highest level, it means a spirituality based upon accomplishment and attainment, and the constant desire for spiritual experiences. This is the story of our society. We have long ago lost the symbolic approach to life, as we have lost a truly religious perspective. Today, we are looking desperately for symbolic meaning in a world based on quantity.

Yet there is a solution. Not a way back, but a way through the numerical to something higher. When one looks at the Torah as a spiritual document deeply concerned with the unity of God, one is immediately struck by its fascination with numbers. Everything is listed: people, places, dates, chattel. This is especially evident in the Biblical passages describing the building of the *Mishkan*, the portable desert Sanctuary. Six chapters are devoted to its design and construction, which entailed two years of work, three tons of silver and two tons of gold, 600 square yards of curtain, forty-eight standing boards, ninety-six sockets, in addition to incense, oil, skins and dyes. After listing all these details, the Torah relates the moment of its assemblage:

The Temple of Amount

And the Lord spoke to Moses, saying: On the first day of the first month you shall set up the tabernacle of the Tent of Meeting. And you shall put in it the Ark of the Testimony, and hang the veil before the Ark. And you shall bring in the table, and set in order the things upon it; and you shall bring in the candlestick, and light its lamps. And you shall set the altar of gold for incense before the Ark of the Testimony, and put the screen of the door to the tabernacle. And you shall set the altar of the burnt offering before the door of the tabernacle of the Tent of Meeting…

Thus did Moses, according to all that the Lord commanded him, so he did… Then a cloud covered the Tent of Meeting, and the Glory of the Lord filled the tabernacle. And Moses was not able to enter the Tent of Meeting, because the cloud rested on it, and the Glory of the Lord filled the tabernacle. (Exodus 40:1–7, 16, 33–38)

An almost identical scenario is recorded in the Books of the Kings, occurring five centuries later with the building of the Holy Temple in Jerusalem. Again, after four chapters of detailed descriptions, the verses conclude:

And Solomon made all the vessels that belonged to the house of the Lord: the altar of gold, and the table of gold, upon which the showbread was, and the candlesticks of pure gold, five on the right side, and five on the left, before the inner sanctuary, with the flowers, and the lamps, and the tongs of gold, and the bowls and the snuffers, and the basins, and the spoons, and the firepans of pure gold; and the hinges of gold, both for the doors of the inner house, and the most holy place, and for the doors of the outer house, namely, the Temple.

So was ended all the work that King Solomon made for the house of the Lord. And Solomon brought in the things that David his father had dedicated; the silver, and the gold, and the vessels, he put in the treasuries of the house of the Lord... And the priests brought in the Ark of the Covenant of the Lord to its place, into the sanctuary of the house, to the most holy place, under the wings of the Cherubim.

And it came to pass, when the priests came out of the holy place, that the cloud filled the house of the Lord, so that the priests could not stand to minister because of the cloud: for the Glory of the Lord had filled the house.... (1 Kings 7:48-51, 8:6, 10-11)

This is number redeemed! These verses tell us that when the elements of creation are incorporated into a structure with the single goal of serving God, a shift can occur that transforms number into something higher – into a vessel for revelation. Kabbalah teaches that the Temple was a microcosm of creation, in which all the components worked together to reveal the will of God. It also compares the Temple to the human body, with the Divine Presence filling it like a soul. What is implied here is a harmony so great that it can only be defined by the word "organism." For the nature of an organism is that it exists only through the unity of its parts, with each part deriving life only to the degree that it is connected to the whole, and through the whole, something greater than all the parts – soul – becomes revealed.

Rabbi Adin Steinsaltz sees this as an integral aspect of entire Torah:

> The system of the *mitzvos* [commandments] constitutes the design for a coherent harmony, its separate com-

ponents being like the instruments of an orchestra. So vast is the harmony to be created by this orchestra that it includes the whole world and promises the perfecting of the world. Seeing the *mitzvos* in this light, one may understand on the one hand, the need for so great a number of details and, on the other, the denial of any exclusive emphasis on any one detail or aspect of life. The *mitzvos* as a system include all of life, from the time one opens one's eyes in the morning until one goes to sleep, from the day of birth to the last breath.

This is the great mystery at the heart of all true religious traditions: the fallen state of number is redeemed precisely in terms of its flaw, and out of diversity, the greatest unity can emerge. Likewise, on the individual level, when a person devotes all of his talents and resources to the service of the spirit, he can be lifted above his own divided nature and produce in himself something much more whole. Even when his practice is based upon selfish motivations, the very act of moving in a Godward direction can deliver him from his flaws. "Let a person study Torah even for self-centered reasons, for eventually this will lead him to study it selflessly," says the Talmud.

This brings us to our present time. Never in human history has there been a generation more obsessed with achievement and acquisition, with number and detail. Never have people had to deal with so much information and specificity of knowledge. Logically, this should result in a fragmentation of society and a decreased ability for human beings to interact. Yet, we see the opposite occurring; there has never been a greater potential for communication between people and ideas, never have distant territories been more interdependent.

These two contrasting forces are propelling our civilization forward. Certainly, in all our hearts, we dream that their interaction will produce a larger whole – an era of world peace and harmony. All of creation is God's Temple, and every individual can be a holy vessel. When all the parts have been put into place, God's glory can once more fill His house. However, without a clear statement of this goal, without the basic religious perspective that leads to transcendence, it is almost unthinkable that this should occur. For the self is valid as a framework of meaning only when it operates in the symbolic mode. When it finds meaning in the realm of number, in its own strength and autonomy, there is no limit to its potential for avarice and destructiveness. Only within the context of a religious system, where self-interests are harnessed as motivation for personal growth and transformation, can the fallen world of number be redeemed. If our society is to reach its goal, we must re-envision human life and social organization in terms of cooperation and community – as an organism moving toward God – rather than in terms of quantification, with the egoism and competition that result.

Day by day, I am driven by forces that I do not understand – striving to be better, longing for God, moving toward a goal that I cannot foresee. Sometimes, a person can be so obsessed with the parts that he does not see the whole he is slowly building. Perhaps, it is precisely the search for the symbolic in the world of amount that transforms number into something higher. My deepest hope is that before the last day, God will assemble the disparate pieces of my life into a structure that reveals His will. "And the Lord, whom

The Temple of Amount

you seek, will come suddenly into His Temple" (Malachi 3:1). For in the end, only God can create this whole, shining His light from above to bring unity out of diversity. "Who can bring the pure out of the impure?" asks the prophet. "Only the One" (Job 14:4).

❧

> This is something the human mind cannot comprehend, how the world of multiplicity derives from God's simple unity. For God, in His wisdom, creates countless species, each one unique, yet all deriving from His perfect Oneness.
>
> Nevertheless, it is precisely by means of the multiplicity of creation that we can come to know God. For this is the entire purpose of creation; yet this is something we cannot understand. We have only to rely upon our faith.
>
> R. Nosson of Breslov
> *Likutey Halachos, Kelai Behemah* 4:1

The Untouched Oil

To say that life was hard for the residents of the Lower East Side was to do them an injustice. The streets of New York were not paved with gold, as they had been led to believe: their stones were cold and hard. No work, no money, no opportunity. Grown men ate portions of food too small for children, and children ate much less. For every one job that opened up, fifty new immigrants streamed off Ellis Island. Life was indeed hard, but hardest of all for those Jews who still clung to the religion of their forefathers. Monday morning out on the streets looking for work – take what you can get – then on Friday afternoon came the inevitable question, "Are you coming in tomorrow?" "No." "Then don't come in next Monday." This is how it went, week after week. Not many held on, not even the pious.

Yaakov Cohen was one of these faithful. A descendant of a long line of distinguished rabbis, he could recite his family tree with ease. Furthermore, he was a Kohen, a Priest, another unending source of pride. He often dreamt of the day when the Holy Temple in Jerusalem would be rebuilt, and how he and his children would serve there. In his small town in Poland he was a prominent figure. His small grocery provided a modest living for his wife and four sons, but his real life centered around the community. He was the *gabbai* of the *shul*, ran a soup kitchen for the needy, gave classes to young married men, and every Friday afternoon, lit the golden candelabra in the synagogue, to welcome the oncoming Shabbos. He was a good Jew, and no one could question his faith.

But America was different. There were many Yaakov Cohens here, many other pious, but they had fallen before the onslaughts of hunger, sickness, and cold winter nights. Yaakov, like the others, had come with the dream of building a better life, and like so many others, he found his dream difficult to fulfill. His problem was accentuated by his appearance – his beard and *peyos* clearly labeled him a "*Shomer Shabbos*," and employers would hardly look at him. What could poor Yaakov do? Compromise crept in slowly. The *peyos* eventually went. The beard was trimmed, shorter and shorter, until it too was gone. But as for the Holy Shabbos, he would not touch that, not even a hair.

However, the hunger of winter was the hardest of all, and Yaakov could find no work. Nothing. He walked the streets, peered into store windows, eavesdropped on the conversations of well-fed businessmen on street corners. Maybe, maybe... Then one day he spied a little notice besides a drugstore telephone: "Bookkeeper wanted. Inquire 11-15 Delancey St., second floor." Yaakov pulled down the note and stuffed it into his pocket. Moments later, he was ushered into a small office. A fat man with a foul-smelling cigar showed him his job. "Here are the books. These are the entries. Here is what you write. This is what you add. It's a lot of work, and it must be done on time." Yaakov nodded, acceptingly. "And one more thing," the fat man added, "of course you work Saturdays." Yaakov looked down. He rubbed his dry, cracking hands, he stared at his worn, peeling shoes. He nodded, acceptingly.

CHANGES

Life changed after that, for better and for worse. Yes, there was food for Yaakov's family, but now, he hardly saw them. Off to work early in the morning, back late at night, and how many nights did he sleep at his desk? He found that if he worked very hard, he could silence the small nagging voice within him. Meanwhile, his sons were growing up. Without a strong father-figure to guide them, their own commitment to Torah was becoming lax, and New York offered many distractions for these strong, young men. Only Yaakov's youngest son, Ephraim, maintained his childish faith. Still only nine-years old, he enjoyed reading Psalms, or studying Torah in the back rows of the corner *shtiebel*. Ephraim was very young when his family came to America. He did not remember Poland, and his memories of his father before his transformation were poignant, but fleeting. Still, he read the *Chumash*, and the *Midrashim*, and dreamt of a golden Temple in a holy land where Priests served the living God. One day, he and his family would be there.

Time passed. Yaakov the Cohen became thin. Leaning over his books, his eyes became weak. He did not observe much of anything these days, and he would not remember the past.

It was a cold afternoon in late November. Ephraim Cohen was searching through his parent's bedroom closet, as children often do. Perhaps he was looking for a hidden treasure, or, since Chanukah was less than a week away, he may have been searching for a flask of pure untouched olive oil. He found something just as good.

Among some old papers, an expired passport, a birth certificate, and some tattered greeting cards, he found an old black and white photo of a young boy wearing a pair of *tefillin*. The boy's face shone with strength and intelligence, and he stood with a pride undimmed in the faded print. On the back was written the date – 1901.

Ephraim brought the photo to his mother. "Mother, who is this?" he asked. His mother stared at it long; she turned it over, then over again. "I believe this is your father on his bar-mitzvah day," she sighed. "Is this father? Is this really father?" he said in disbelief. Ephraim ran down to the street where his oldest brother was unloading a wagon. "Shimi," he said, "who is this?" He examined the photo, and recognized something of that same look in his own little brother's eyes. "This is father," he answered softly.

That night, the brothers sat around the kitchen table and sighed, passing the photo back and forth. "This is father. What has happened to him? What has happened to us? We must do something to help."

Suddenly, Shimon, the oldest, spoke up. "I have an idea," he said. He ran to the hall closet and began shifting through the old newspapers, the yellowing tablecloths. After a moment he pulled out a faded blue cloth bag – his father's *tefillin*. Long unused, they had sat there patiently waiting. He ran back to his brothers, holding up his prize.

That night, a Wednesday, as Yaakov slept at his accounting desk, his oldest son quietly entered the office and placed the *tefillin* on the table before him.

When Yaakov awoke in the morning, he could not believe his eyes. It was as though a dream of the past had floated down into reality. He gently picked up the bag and smiled as he examined the gold and silver embroidery on the blue velvet. He put his hand inside and felt the smooth leather straps. What is written in *tefillin*? the Talmud asks. "Hear, Oh Israel, the Lord is our God, the Lord is One." And what is written in God's *tefillin*? "Who is like Your people, Israel, a one nation on earth." Yaakov returned to his accounting, but throughout the day, as he inscribed numbers with his right hand, his left hand rested comfortably on the *tefillin* bag before him.

That night Yaakov again fell asleep at his accounting desk and in the still darkness, his second son, Nachum, slipped into the room and quietly laid his father's *tallis* in front of him.

When Yaakov awoke that next morning, a Friday, he blinked in disbelief. "What is going on here?" he thought. "Where did this come from? Is this real?" He rubbed the yellowing wool, he fingered the fraying *tzitzis*. It was real. He spread out the *tallis*. It was worn and moth-eaten, a little like Yaakov himself. Still, there was a certain dignity to it. He remembered the High Holidays services, and how, even as a child, he would stand at the front of the synagogue, *tallis* over his head and arms, and bless the people: "May God bless you and protect you. May God shine His face upon you and be gracious to you. May God lift His face to you, and bestow upon you peace." He had always meant it, as well.

"It's cold in here," he told himself, "Maybe this will keep me warm." He wrapped himself in the old *tallis* and strangely, it *did* keep him warm. He bent over his work and continued, the ragged *tallis* around his shoulders, his left hand resting upon the *tefillin* bag.

Sometime towards dusk, Yaakov laid his head upon his arm and fell asleep. When he awoke it was already night. He looked up and saw what appeared to be two flaming angels hovering in the darkness before him. He blinked, rubbed his eyes, and beheld two Shabbos candles burning brightly on his desk. While he had slept, his third son had placed them there, made the blessing over the Shabbos, and left. Yaakov gave a great shudder. A flood of memories overwhelmed him. "Shabbos," he whispered to himself, "Shabbos, Shabbos."

Yaakov stared into those lights. He sat unmoving for hours as they slowly burned down. In those holy Shabbos lights he saw many things. He saw his own wife lighting Shabbos candles back in their home in Poland. He saw his mother, too, as she would pray for her family before the Shabbos lights, and his ruddy cheeked grandmother kindling the lights, as well. Yaakov saw the oil lamps of the *Beis HaMidrash*, where scholars studied the holy Torah deep into the night. And he saw the Shabbos lights of his own *shul*, that he, himself, once lit.

His vision went back. He saw the lights that Jews had lit for thousands of years – a million *Chanukiot* in a million homes. He saw the *Kohen Gadol* tending the lights of the holy Menorah in the Sanctuary. The wars of the Chashmonaim, as they fought to reclaim their religion. He saw the countless Jews whose lives had ended in flames because they had refused to abandon their Torah. And, at the very end, before the candles died out, as they flickered their last, dull, orange and blue flame, he saw the destruction of Jerusalem, the burning of the *Beis HaMikdash*, and the beginning of the long, dark exile.

Yaakov did not return home that night, nor Shabbos by day, nor *motzaei* Shabbos, nor Sunday. And Sunday night was the first night of Chanukah.

In their small apartment, his four sons sat anxiously looking out the window. In their hands was a small candle that would serve as an impoverished Menorah. They watched the darkening horizon, waiting for the proper moment in which to light, but silently, their eyes scanned the streets, searching for something else. Darkness fell, the stars would soon appear.

"We may as well begin," Shimon, the oldest, finally said.

At that moment, from down below on the street, they heard a call. "Shimon, Nachum, Tzvi, Ephraim. Come down!" It was their father! Like sparks from a bonfire they flew out the door and down the steps.

Standing in front of the house was Yaakov. Beside the door, in a small glass case, was a beautiful gold-colored Menorah. "My boys, my dear boys," he said, "you saved me. You did. You were the angels that brought about my deliverance. I've made many mistakes, I'll admit them, but from now on things will be different." His eyes were wet with tears. "Now, come, who will help me light the Menorah? We have only one candle tonight."

Shimon, the oldest, spoke up first. "Me, Father, because I brought you your *tefillin*, it was really my idea." "You're right, my son, and it was a beautiful idea. It's what woke me up from my sleep." Nachum stepped forward. "Father, I brought you your *tallis*." "Yes, my son, that too was important. It warmed my very soul." "Father," said Tzvi, "I lit the Shabbos candles." "Tzvi, that was most precious gift of all." He turned to Ephraim, the youngest. "What about you, Ephraim? What did you do?" "Nothing, father. Only I... I found an old photo of you in the closet, and I went around asking everyone, 'Is this father? Is this father?'"

His father paused. "Then to you, Ephraim, I owe the most. Because you cared enough to ask about me, and a man is never completely lost as long as someone cares about him. Your words woke up every one of us." He took Ephraim's hand. "Come boys, let us light the Menorah with your little brother, Ephraim." The brothers gathered around as Yaakov bent forward to light the Menorah, and there was joy in their hearts, because they knew their father had returned.

The Untouched Oil

A king had two sons. Once, during a battle, one of his sons was taken captive. However, after a long time and great effort, he managed to escape and return to his father. There is no question that the joy that this son feels upon returning home is much greater than that of his brother, who never left his father's side. For it was only by being held in captivity that he realized how much he loved his father, and how much he yearned for him.

BAAL SHEM TOV

If a person knew that everything is from God – both the good and the bad – he would never fear anything. This is like a father who dons a costume in order to frighten his young son. The child is scared at first, though once he realizes that it is his father, he cries in a loud voice, "Father, father!" Then, the father's heart fills with love for his child and he removes his disguise.

Likewise, if a person truly knew that all his suffering was actually his Heavenly Father in disguise, looking to see if His son recognizes Him, his pain would be eased. One who doesn't realize this, however, searches for earthly remedies, for he cannot free himself of his suffering.

BAAL SHEM TOV

❧ RESPONSIBILITY ☙

*The tablets were the work of God and
the writing was the writing of God;
freedom was inscribed on the tablets.*

– Exodus 32:16

GOING BACK TO THE BEGINNING OF MY JOURney (and the first essay, above), I've found that same inclination that kept me out of a monastery – the desire to find God in the world – also changed the way I think about spirituality. That is, it moved from being a solely personal matter to being a universal one. In Chasidus, at least, these two approaches are usually intertwined. Fixing oneself means fixing the world, and taking responsibility for the world ultimately influences every action a person can take.

The Age of Tikkun

There is a word that is repeated throughout history. It is spoken in times of peace, when society builds hopefully for the future, and in times of war, when men struggle for the present; it captures the best of our dreams and aspirations. Judaism refers to it often, for it is at the heart of all her laws and customs, and finds expression in nearly every aspect of the religious life. It is the goal of both the legalist and the mystic, of both leaders and the simple man seeking quietude. The word is *Tikkun*.

Tikkun has several connotations: correction, restoration, reform. Most often, it is used in the phrase *tikkun olam*, usually translated as "repairing the world." It conveys a sense of putting things right, of promoting harmony and integration among the various elements of creation and peace among humanity. Tikkun is understood to be the goal of all the Torah's commandments: "The *mitzvos* were only given to purify the world," says the Midrash. It manifests itself on all levels of society, whether one works in the broad arena of the public good, or merely tries to refine one's own life, both contribute to the same goal of *tikkun olam*. Ultimately, *tikkun* means imbuing the creation with such a profound sense of life and spirit that the entire world becomes a vessel for Revelation. In that sense, *tikkun* also means "healing," for it means returning to the world its soul.

This was humanity's role from the very beginning. It was for this reason that God declared: "Let us make humankind in Our image, after Our likeness: and let them have dominion over the fish of the sea, and over the birds of the air, and over the cattle, and over all the earth..." (Genesis 1:26). This dominion is not a form of control or manipulation; rather it is a type of stewardship, leading all the parts to a greater whole. The word "dominion" in this verse, *vayerdu*, is related to the word "to go down," just as a greater person must descend to see to the needs of a lower one, for *tikkun* is always concerned with raising up that which is fallen.

According to the Kabbalah, when God first formed the universe, He left it incomplete, one step away from Divinity. Adam was supposed to close the circle and finish the *tikkun*. But when he sinned in the Garden, rather than uplifting the world, he plunged it further into darkness, making the process of repair so much harder. There is a Kabbalistic teaching that says that as a direct result of Adam's sin, the Children of Israel, many centuries later, would be forced to descend into Egypt to experience bondage and deliverance; for there is a direct relationship between the act of *tikkun* and the movement from slavery to freedom.

It has been noted that the Torah, as a book of law, never speaks in terms of rights; all its laws are phrased in the language of responsibilities – to one's family, one's community, or to God. Though the law is preeminently concerned with the welfare of the poor and the underprivileged, it nonetheless speaks only of our obligations. However, there is at least one area in which the law does allude to human rights: in the treatment of slaves and indentured servants. Even in ancient times, when slavery was common, the Torah protected their welfare. Of the rights of a slave, the verse states, "It shall be good for him with you" (Deuteronomy 15:16). According to the Talmud, this means that a slave must be fed and clothed well, he must not be overworked, embarrassed or belittled in any way, and if his master abuses him physically, he is allowed to go free.

The Torah is making a subtle point, that the difference between rights and responsibilities is the difference between slavery and freedom. For a free man is not defined by the rights he deserves, but by the responsibilities that he bears. Freedom is not an end unto itself, to be the focus of legislation; it is a means to something greater, to bring the world to perfection. Only a person under the subjugation of another needs rights, but since the Torah views man as intrinsically free, it makes him responsible for others, and for the entire world.

In the mystical teachings of Chasidus, the concepts of slavery and freedom are understood on a deeper level – as states of consciousness. "We were slaves to Pharaoh in Egypt, and the Lord our God took us out from there," begins the Passover Hagaddah. The essence of slavery is not physical subjugation or restricted movement, but a limited state of consciousness in which the mind cannot recognize the truth of God in the present moment but sees only a facade of illusions and fantasies projected by the ego and the lower inclinations. Slavery means living in a world of dreams, whereas true freedom means relating to the world as it exists before us now, as an emanation from God, with all its potential for becoming a vessel for holiness. The First Commandment states, "I am the Lord Your God who took you out of Egypt..." (Exodus 20:2). That is, the deliverance from bondage is precisely that which leads us to a perception of the "Lord our God." One who attains this state of consciousness is free, even when he is physically restrained, for he is at every moment attached to the Divine. Whereas even a person with autonomy of movement is enslaved, so long as he cannot liberate himself from the influence of his fantasies and lower self.

Thus, the act of *tikkun* is not merely an act of repairing the world, but of repairing the consciousness, until we can clearly see what needs to be done in this world. It means freeing ourselves from personal interests and biases in order to serve the needs of the present moment. For it is in *this* moment, with all its problems and deficiencies, that God reveals Himself to us. Freedom means giving to others, even when the deed is unfulfilling, or putting aside one's own interests for the sake of a greater good. In a word, it means the willingness to sacrifice for the highest vision of goodness and truth. This is the process of both individual and universal redemption. Chasidus teaches that when all the illusions of the world have finally been exhausted, history will have reached its end, and the world will reach its *tikkun*.

Seen in this light, the concepts of slavery and freedom apply to our generation as well. Never in history have these two opposites been stronger: the unbridled reign of the imagination fostered by our media culture, versus the need for the most sober and realistic world view in the face of our great power for destruction; our potential to bring the world to perfection versus our ability to totally annihilate it. We have finally fulfilled the verse, "You have made [man] a little less than the angels... You have given him dominion over the works of Your hands; You have put all things under his feet: all sheep and oxen, the beasts of the field; the birds of the sky, and the fish of the sea" (Psalms 8:6-9). We must remember, with everything that we do, that this means stewardship over the earth, with the goal of bringing it to perfection. Thus, even while we examine other traditions for alternative paradigms of society – Native American, Aborigine, earth religions – we must realize that humankind, having mastered so much of this planet, will never return to those models. And since we will never relinquish our control, we have no choice but to learn to use it properly.

The question now is how to become free, how to take responsibility for all of our actions. For we can no longer afford to be slaves to our illusions, ignoring the repercussions of our acts. God created Adam and placed him in the Garden "to serve it and to protect it" (Genesis 2:15). The Kabbalah teaches that Adam was supposed to repair the world on the very first day of his creation. Yet he failed to take responsibility for the earth, insisting instead on his right to eat from every tree in the Garden. But though he fell, the job of *tikkun* remains the same, only now it has to be performed by countless individuals over thousands of years, for the soul of Adam was divided and spread out over time.

That means that every human being, on whatever level of society, has something to fix, something to heal, some way in which to use the gift of their life for a higher purpose, correctly, responsibly. The Midrash says that while Adam still lay silent on the ground, God showed him all the generations that would emerge from him. Some were derived from his head, some from his heart, some from his feet. Each person has his place and his role; together we constitute the body of Adam. Likewise, when the Torah speaks of responsibilities, it is not just addressing those in power. The underprivileged also have obligations, and according to Jewish Law, even the beggar on the street must give charity to those worse off than him. By doing so, he too contributes to the repair of the world, within his own limited sphere of influence.

Now we stand on the threshold of a new millennium. So many ages have already passed before us, from the Classical Age to the Age of Technology, from the Romantic period to the Post-Modern age. Each one has left its mark upon the world; some have done it harm. What age will we now be facing?

We must enter the Age of *Tikkun*, of Healing – for the damage we have done to ourselves and the world over the past centuries, and because the earth still waits to fulfill its purpose. We exist in this world in order to fix and uplift, and have a responsibility to all of creation. The Midrash says that when God created Adam, He took him around the Garden of Eden and showed him all the trees. "Do you see My handiwork, how beautiful and choice it is? Be careful not to ruin and destroy My world, for if you do, there will be no one after you to repair it." This command still applies to us. We must not despair in the face of the challenge, but only see our great potential for healing. May God help us finally fulfill what we are meant to do on this earth.

A Single Glance

A true story

The first thing young Moshe Yitzchok did upon arriving in Vienna was to change his name; the second was to enroll in an academy of secular studies. Neither step would have pleased his parents, but it would be a long time before they found out. Moshe Yitzchok had been traveling for several years now and his contact with them during that time had been minimal. Of course he still loved them and had many fond memories of his childhood, but life had carried him to a place where they could not go.

Moshe Yitzchok had grown up in the small Polish town of Linden. He had received a traditional Jewish education and his father had tried hard to instill in him an appreciation for his religious heritage. But young Moshe's heart was drawn to something else – to a wider world, to new ways of thinking and acting. The ghetto walls were collapsing, and new possibilities were opening themselves to the Jews. Moshe read avidly, and was drawn to philosophy and science. As soon as he was old enough, he left Linden and began to travel. Slowly his outer appearance adapted to the new world in which he found himself, and likewise did his beliefs. How archaic were the superstitions of his parents, how unsuited to the modern world in which he now lived!

Finally, Moshe Yitzhak arrived in Vienna. He changed his name to Moses, and enrolled in a conservatory. Because he was bright, he quickly made up for years of lost studies. And as he progressed, he took on more and more of the local customs. It was not long before he lost all semblance of a small-town Jewish boy. On finishing his studies, he decided to pursue a career in medicine. He enrolled in university and quickly rose in prominence. After receiving his degree, he began to work as a surgeon in the Central Vienna Hospital. He was admired for his skill and expertise; his Jewishness was never an issue.

Rabbi Yehoshua Rokeach, the Grand-Rabbi of Belz, was one of the leaders of European Jewry. From his Chasidic court in Galicia, his influence spread throughout Europe. In 1855, at the age of thirty, he had inherited his father's place as Rebbe, and for nearly forty years, he led his flock with wisdom and insight. He was not only a scholar of Torah, but a man of the world, engaged in politics and every area of communal activity. Like his father, he was a fierce antagonist of the *Haskalah*, the "Enlightenment" movement that was stealing so many European Jews away from their heritage.

Now, at only sixty-nine years of age, he was showing serious signs of weakness. A strange illness gripped his body, and though outwardly, he remained positive and encouraging, inwardly he suffered terribly. He had visited nearly every doctor in Galicia, but none could offer him a cure. His chasidim were even more concerned, for the Rebbe had hinted to them that soon, his guiding presence would no longer be available to lead them.

A Single Glance

When his condition deteriorated further, his followers pressed him to travel to Vienna, for treatment by Europe's finest doctors. The trip from Galicia was difficult, and the Rebbe arrived weak and depleted. At the Central Vienna Hospital, the experts assessed his condition – he would need a major operation as soon as possible, and even then, the chances of his recovery were slim. The operation was scheduled for one o'clock the following afternoon. The chasidim spent that entire morning fasting and praying for their leader's welfare.

At about a quarter to one, the Rebbe was brought into the operating room. Before separating from his chasidim, he spoke to them privately. He told them not to fear, that God would not abandon them, that they needed only to follow the path he set for them to speed the final redemption. Then, as the attendant wheeled him away, the Rebbe closed his eyes and went deep inside of himself. His face was still; his lips were uttering a silent prayer.

The doctors in the operating room were all ready. They were only waiting for the anesthesiologist to arrive. Moses stood among them, towards the back. When the Rebbe was wheeled in, Moses was struck by his beauty – such a love and gentleness radiated from his pale face. The room was quiet; the Rebbe was in another place.

Suddenly, the Rebbe opened his eyes and began to survey the doctors who surrounded him. It was as though he was looking for something familiar that he sensed in the room. Finally, he noticed the young doctor standing beside the wall.

"Doctor, what is your name?" he asked. Moses was taken aback by the sudden, personal call.

"Moses Wilner," he answered.

"Moses, are you Jewish?" the Rebbe asked gently.

Moses coughed. He nodded his head in acknowledgement.

The Rebbe continued. "Moses, do you believe in the Creator and Ruler of the world?"

Moses' face went red. What a question! He wanted to leave the room, to avoid the stares of his colleagues – but the operation was about to begin. He paused a moment. "Yes, Rebbe, I do," he answered.

The other doctors in the room were bewildered. They looked on in amazement as a strange dialogue began to unfold between patient and doctor. The Rebbe, however, paid them no attention. All his concentration was focused upon the young Jewish doctor who had turned his back on his faith.

"And in our righteous Messiah, who is ready to come at any moment and redeem his people from exile, do you believe in him too, Moses?"

Moses was dead still. There was no place to hide. He closed his eyes from the Rebbe's enquiring gaze and tried to formulate an answer. The words came out slowly.

"Ah, hmm, you see, Rebbe, I believe in the historical process, that mankind is gradually progressing. One day, there will come a time of world peace, and then our people will experience their redemption and find a place among the nations of the world. But I do not believe that this will come about through the influence of one man, the Messiah, who will somehow transform all of humanity. That strikes me as completely impossible."

The Rebbe of Belz was silent. Then, suddenly, he turned his whole head to face the young doctor. His glance was penetrating.

A Single Glance

For the first time, Moses looked directly into his eyes – they were so deep, so full of wisdom; kind but strong, gentle but intense. Moses was transfixed. He felt himself being drawn into the Rebbe's gaze, as though it contained some profound secret. Then, in his own mind, hidden clambers of memory slowly began to open. Memories of a forgotten past, of his childhood and his parents' home, beautiful memories – and disturbing ones. Powerful emotions surged through him: Elation, ecstasy, fear, longing. The Rebbe's eyes grabbed him, they were touching his soul. Enough! He had to look away. Too much was being revealed, emotions that he could not bear to face.

He tried to avert his gaze; but he could not. He tried to turn his head, but it was impossible. It was as though he was gripped by the Rebbe's gaze. Moses' face became white, then red, then white again. The veins on his neck began to protrude. His body started to shake, his hands to tremble.

The other doctors stared on in amazement. A storm was raging inside their colleague, though they could not perceive its source. Moses gasped for air. All his efforts to calm himself failed, which only increased his panic. The Rebbe held him firmly with his eyes, they penetrated to his depths. The young doctor began to softly cry.

Another moment passed, and then the Rebbe removed his gaze from him. Moses felt his composition slowly returning. Afterward, the Rebbe looked at him once again. This time his eyes were gentle, comforting.

"Moses, now do you believe that one person can influence another with a single glance alone? That is exactly how it will be when the Messiah comes. God has chosen him to lead the world to perfection. He will return all people from their erroneous ways."

RESPONSIBILITY

Moses lowered his eyes and nodded in submission. "The Rebbe is right, and I was mistaken," he said in a whisper.

The anesthesiologist had already arrived and in a few moments, the Rebbe was asleep. The operation lasted several hours, and was a success. Throughout Europe, chasidim rejoiced.

Two weeks passed, and the Rebbe recuperated in the hospital. During that time, an air of sanctity and peace rested upon the building. Finally, he left Vienna to return home. On the train-ride back to Galicia, Rabbi Yehoshua Rokeach, the Grand-Rabbi of Belz, passed away. He was surrounded by a small group of chasidim at the time. Among them was a young doctor named Moshe Yitzchok Wilner, who was returning home to recover a treasure he had long ago left behind.

A Single Glance

When one Jew loves another, he can uplift him spiritually. This is like a person who is invited to dine with the king, but replies, "I don't want to go unless my friend comes with me." Similarly, if two Jews form a bond of love, they can each say. "I don't want to go unless my friend is with me." This applies to every Jew; it is the inner meaning of the Covenant. And to the degree that a person is part of this Covenant, he can bring the entire world to perfection.

R. NOSSON DOVID OF SHIDLOVITZ
Imrei Binah, Behar

God only loves one who loves the Jewish people, and the more a person loves his fellow Jew, the greater is the love God showers upon him.

R. MOSHE CHAIM LUZZATTO
Mesilas Yeshorim 19

Glossary

Ahavas Yisroel – Love for one's fellow Jews; as enjoined by the Torah's precept "Love your fellow as yourself" (Leviticus 19:18).

Avodas Hashem – The service of God, such as prayer, Torah study, *mitzvos* and good deeds.

Ba'al Teshuvah – Literally, a "Master of Return." One who returns to Jewish observance after a falling away, or after having grown up non-observant.

Baruch Hashem – Thank God! (Literally: "Blessed is God!")

Beis HaMidrash – A study hall of Torah.

Bikurim – The first fruits, offered in the Temple in Jerusalem. Based on Exodus 23:19; 34:26, Numbers 15:17–21; 18:12–13; and Deuteronomy 26:1–11.

Binah – "Understanding." The second intellectual *sefirah* on the Kabbalistic Tree of Life.

Bitachon – Trust in God.

Breslov – A Chasidic group started by Rabbi Nachman of Breslov.

Chanukiah – Another word for a menorah, the eight-branched candelabra used on Chanukah.

Chareidi – A general reference to "ultra-orthodox" Jews. Literally, "those who tremble" at the word of God.

Chasidus – "Chasidism," in English. A popular, Jewish spiritual revivalist movement of 18th century Eastern Europe, with roots in Kabbalistic teachings, started by Rabbi Yisroel Baal Shem Tov.

Chavrusah (Chavrusos) – A study-partner in yeshivah.

Chesed – "Loving-kindness." The fourth of the ten *sefirot* on the Kabbalistic Tree of Life, and the first of the emotive attributes.

Chidushei Torah – Original Torah insights and interpretations.

Chochmah – "Wisdom." The second of the *sefirot* on the Kabbalistic Tree of Life, and first of the three intellectual attributes.

Chumash – The Five Books of Moses.

Devekus – Spiritual attachment to God, from the Hebrew root *devek* – to cleave to.

Gabbai – The synagogue attendant who oversees services and determines which congregants receive honors during the Torah reading.

Gan Eden – The Garden of Eden.

Gemara – The Talmud.

Gevurah – "Strength." The fifth *sefirah* in the Kabbalistic Tree of Life, and the second of the emotive attributes. It is positioned below *Binah* and across from *Chesed*.

Halacha – Jewish law. Literally, "the way to walk."

Hod – "Majesty" or "Glory." The eighth *sefirah* of the Kabbalistic Tree of Life.

Ikkar – "The main thing," as opposed to *tafel* – a secondary thing.

Kabbalah – The Jewish mystical tradition, including both meditative practices and metaphysical theories.

Kesser – "Crown." The first of the ten Sefirot in the Kabbalistic Tree of Life. It is the intermediary point between the God's Infinite Light and the finite creation.

Glossary

Kippah (kippot) – The small, round head covering worn by observant Jewish males. Also known as a yarmulke.

Kohen Gadol – The High Priest, who served in the Holy Temple in Jerusalem.

Kotel – The Western Wall in Jerusalem.

Krias Shema – The declaration of God's unity: "Here, O Israel, the Lord is our God, the Lord is One" (Deuteronomy 6:4).

Maggid – A religious preacher and storyteller.

Malchus – The tenth and lowest *sefirah* on the Kabbalistic Tree of Life, whose purpose it is to receive and reveal the Divine energy that flows into it from Above. Often considered feminine in nature.

Midrash (Midrashim) – Rabbinic, homiletic commentary on the Torah.

Mikvah – A large bath or pool of water used for ritual purification.

Mishkan – The portable sanctuary used by the Israelites during their desert wanderings, as described in Exodus 25–31 and 35–40.

Mitzvah – Specifically, one of the 613 commandments found in the Torah. Colloquially, any good deed.

Moshiach – The Messiah. Literally, "the anointed one."

Motzaei Shabbos – Saturday night, after the conclusion of the Shabbos.

Nes – A miracle. Also, a sign.

Niggun – A Jewish melody, often without words.

Parshah – The weekly Torah portion, read aloud in synagogue each Shabbos morning.

Peyos – Sidecurls, often worn long by chasidim. Based on Leviticus 19:27: "You shall not round off the corners of your head."

Rabbeinu – Hebrew for "our Rabbi."

Reb – A Yiddish honorific traditionally used for Orthodox Jewish men; not a rabbinic title, but more the equivalent of the English "Mister."

Rebbe – Yiddish for "Rabbi," which means "master, teacher, or mentor." Within the Chasidic movement, it usually refers to the leader or "Grand Rabbi" of each particular sect.

Ruach hakodesh – "Holy spirit." A state of spiritual enlightenment somewhat akin to prophecy.

Seder – A study period in a yeshiva, such as "morning *seder*" or "afternoon *seder*."

Sefer – Hebrew for "book," usually referring to books with religious content.

Sefiros – The ten Divine emanations through which God creates and directs the creation – from the spiritual worlds down to this physical one.

Segulah – a protective or beneficial charm or ritual from the Kabbalistic or Talmudic tradition.

Shechinah – The Divine presence hidden within reality, and especially, within the human soul. Generally defined as having feminine attributes, inasmuch as it receives, processes and reveals God's light.

Shiurim – Torah classes and lectures.

Shlit"a – An acronym for the words "**Sheyikhye Lirot Yamim Tovim Arukim/Amen**" – "May he live a good long life" or "May he live a good life, Amen." Usually given to a revered rabbi or teacher and written after the name.

Shochet – A ritual slaughterer or fowl and/or kine.

Sholom Aleichem – The common Yiddish greeting. Literally, "peace upon you."

Shomer Shabbos – A person who observes the Shabbos, according to *halacha*.

Glossary

Shtiebel – Yiddish for "a little house." A colloquialism for a local synagogue.

Shul – Another Yiddish term for a synagogue (akin to the German *Schule*, "school").

Siddur – A Jewish prayerbook.

Simchas Torah – A Jewish holiday celebrating the conclusion of the annual cycle of public Torah readings and the beginning of a new cycle. In Israel, it is observed on the holiday of Shemini Atzeres, which immediately follows the festival of Sukkot. In the Diaspora, it is observed on the day following Shemini Atzeres.

Tafel – Hebrew for "ancillary," "of secondary importance."

Tallis – A prayer shawl.

Talmidei chachamim – Torah scholars.

Tefillin – Phylacteries. Black leather boxes strapped to the arm and head during weekday morning prayers, and containing parchment inscribed with Biblical verses.

Teshuva – Repentance.

Tiferes – The sixth *sefirah* in the Kabbalistic Tree of Life. Literally meaning "beauty," but also associated with the traits of balance, integration and compassion.

Tikkun – Rectification, repair, perfecting.

Tikkun HaKlali – Ten specific Psalms, identified by Rabbi Nachman of Breslov, with a mystical, efficacious power to heal spiritual blemishes, particularly those caused by sexual impurity.

Tish – Yiddish for "table." In Chasidic culture, it stands for the Friday night gathering of chasidim to sing together, hear Torah from their Rebbe and observe his behavior, especially in the mundane activities of eating and drinking.

Tisha b'Av – The ninth of the Hebrew month of Av. The day

commemorating the destruction of the First and Second Temples in Jerusalem.

Tzaddik (Tzaddikim) – A righteous and holy man. In the Chasidic movement, the Tzaddik is the leader, spiritual guide and focus of the entire community.

Tzedakah – Charity.

Tzitzis – Ritual fringes or tassels worn by observant Jews, attached to the four corners of a *tallis*. From Numbers 15:38.

Yeshivah bachur – A unmarried yeshivah student.

Yesod – "Foundation." The ninth *sefirah* in the Kabbalistic Tree of Life, whose function is to link the upper sefirotic structure to *malchus*, the lowest *sefirah*.

Biographies

R. *Adin Steinsaltz* – A leading Israeli teacher, philosopher and spiritual mentor (b. 1937.) The author of many books on Jewish thought, as well as a Hebrew translation and commentary on the entire Talmud.

R. *Avraham of Trisk* – Son of Rabbi Mordechai Twersky of Chernobyl, and first Rebbe of the Trisker dynasty (1806-1889). Also known as the Trisker Maggid.

R. *Avraham Yeshaya Karelitz* – Popularly known by the name of his magnum opus, *Chazon Ish* (1878-1953). One of the most brilliant and influential Talmudic and halachic scholars of the 20th century, who helped establish the Israeli, charedi yeshiva system.

R. *Avraham Yissachar Dov HaKohen Rabinowitz of Radoshitz* – The second Rebbe of the Radomsk Chasidic dynasty (1843-1892). Also known as the *Chesed L'Avraham*, after the title of his Torah work.

R. *Avraham Yitzchok HaKohen Kook* – Renowned Jewish thinker, Halachist, Kabbalist and Torah scholar (1865-1935). First Ashkenzi chief rabbi of British Mandatory Palestine. He was a prolific author and remains one of the most influential rabbis of the 20th century.

R. *Dov Ber of Chabad* – Dov Ber Schneuri (1773-1827) was the son of Rabbi Shneur Zalman of Liadi, and the second

Chabad Rebbe. He is also known as the "Mitteler Rebbe" ("Middle Rebbe" in Yiddish), being the second of the first three generations of Chabad leaders.

R. *Boruch Meir Yaakov Shochet* – Current Rebbe of the Karlin-Stolin Chasidic group (b. 1954), which dates back to Rabbi Aharon the Great of Karlin, a leading disciple of the Maggid of Mezritch.

R. *Hillel Zeitlin* – A Yiddish and Hebrew writer (1871-1942), born in Korma, Belorussia. He received the education of a Chabad chasid; however, due to a crisis of faith and the influence of the Haskala, he left Jewish observance. He returned to it years later, out of a longing for spirituality, and devoted the rest of his life to writing and outreach. His life experience in both the secular and religious worlds gave him a unique perspective on Chasidic thought. He died in sanctification of God's Name, garbed in *tallis* and *tefillin*, on the way to Treblinka on the eve of Rosh Hashanah, 1942.

R. *Levi Yitzchok of Berditchev* – A third generation Chasidic Master (1740-1809). One of the main disciples of the Maggid of Mezritch, and famous for his love and defense of all Jews.

R. *Menachem Mendel Morgenstern of Kotzk* – Also known as the Kotzker Rebbe (1787-1859). The leading disciple of Rabbi Simcha Bunim of Peshischa, and a powerful and influential Chasidic Rebbe in Poland. He is famous for his sharp and incisive philosophy and sayings, and is considered to be the spiritual founder of Ger Chasidus.

R. *Mordechai Sharabi* – One of the greatest Kabbalists of the twentieth century (1908-1984). Born in Yemen, he moved to Israel, where he established the Kabbalistic yeshiva Nahar Shalom.

Biographies

R. *Moshe ben Maimon* – Maimonides (c. 1135-1204), also known by the acronym Rambam. The most prolific and influential Torah scholar of the Middle Ages, whose writings deal with Jewish philosophy, *halacha*, medicine and more. As the popular saying goes: "From Moshe (Moses, of the Torah) to Moshe (Maimonides) there was none like Moshe."

R. *Moshe Chaim Luzzatto* – Influential Italian rabbi, Kabbalist, philosopher and writer. (1707-1746). Author of *Mesilas Yeshorim* and *Derech Hashem*, among many other important works.

R. *Moshe Cordovero* – One of the most important figures in the history of Kabbalah, and leader of the Tzefat, Israel mystical school (1522-1570). Also known by the acronym, the Ramak.

R. *Moshe Yechiel HaLevi of Ozharov* – Fifth Rebbe in the Ozharov Chasidic dynasty. Author of the multi-volume work *Be'er Moshe* and *Aish Das* (1890-1971).

R. *Nachman of Breslov* – Great-grandson of the Baal Shem Tov, and one of the most influential and original thinkers in the Chasidic movement (1772-1810). Born in the Ukraine, his Chasidic group is named after the town of Breslov (or Bratzlav), where Rabbi Nachman lived for a period. He was the first and only Rebbe in this line of Chasidus, yet the movement has continued to grow until today. He is buried in the Ukrainian town of Uman, where his grave is a site of pilgrimage for both his chasidim and others.

R. *Nosson Sternhartz of Breslov* – Chief disciple and scribe of Rabbi Nachman of Breslov (1780-1844), who devoted his life to preserving and promoting Rabbi Nachman's teachings. An extremely prolific writer, and author of nearly all early Breslov works, including *Likutey Halachos, Likutey Tefilos, Likutey Eitzos,* and more.

R. *Nosson Dovid Rabinowitz of Shidlovitz* – Polish rabbi and founder of a Chasidic court (1814–1865). Grandson of Rabbi Yaakov Yitzchok Rabinowitz – the "Holy Jew" of Peshischa.

Rafael Yitzchak Ephraim Estrin – Rafi Estrin was a Chabad chasid from Providence, Rhode Island (1975–1997). A young man much wiser than his years, he passed away at the age of twenty-two from cystic fibrosis.

R. *Shimshon Barksy* – A descendent of Rabbi Nachman of Breslov and the author of *Eitzos HaMevuoros,* a Yiddish commentary on *Likutey Eitzos.* He was one of the leading Breslov Chasidim in Uman before the Communists took over the country (d. 1935).

R. *Shlomo Carlebach* – Also known as "The Singing Rabbi" (1925–1994). One of the most beloved Jewish personalities of the 20th century. Reb Shlomo was a teacher, storyteller, composer and singer, and is widely considered to have been the most influential Jewish religious songwriter of his time.

R. *Shmuel Schneersohn* – The fourth Rebbe of the Chabad Lubavitch Chasidic dynasty (1834–1882). He was the seventh son of the third Chabad Rebbe, the "Tzemach Tzedek," and father of the fifth Rebbe, Rabbi Sholom Dovber.

R. *Shneur Zalman of Liadi* – A leading disciple of the Maggid of Mezritch, and founder of the Chabad Chasidic movement (1745–1812). One of the greatest Tzaddikim of his time, and author of many scholarly works, both exoteric and esoteric. He is also known as the "Baal HaTanya" after his best known work, *Sefer HaTanya.*

R. *Tzadok HaKohen Rabinowitz of Lublin* – An eight generation

Biographies

Polish Chasidic master (1823-1900), and leading disciple of Rabbi Mordechai Yosef Leiner of Izhbitz (author of the *Mei HaShiloach*). Rabbi Tzadok was one of the most brilliant, prolific, and deepest of the Chasidic writers, whose works shed light on almost every area of Jewish thought.

R. *Tzvi Elimelech of Dinov* – A fourth generation Chasidic master (1783-1841), and disciple of the Seer of Lublin. A prolific author, best known for his work *Bnei Yissoschar*, which is a Chasidic analysis of the months and holidays of the Jewish year.

R. *Yisrael Abuchatzira* – The great Sefardic Kabbalist, also known as the Baba Sali ("Praying Father) (1889-19984). After making *aliyah* to Israel from Morocco, he settled in Netivot, where he devoted his life to helping and praying for the Jewish people.

R. *Yitzchok Eisik Yehudah Yechiel Safrin of Komarno* – One of the most prolific and original writers of the Chasidic movement (1806-1874), especially devoted to expositing the teachings of the Baal Shem Tov. He was raised by his uncle, the Chasidic master, Rabbi Tzvi Hirsch of Zidichov. He was the author of *Heichal HaBrachah* on the Torah, *Otzar HaChaim* on the commandments, and *Zohar Chai* on the Zohar, among many other works.

R. *Yitzchok Kalish of Vorki* – A disciple of the Chasidic master, Rabbi Simcha Bunim of Peshischa, and first Rebbe of Vorki Chasidic dynasty (1779-1848).

R. *Yosef of Turchin* – Son of Rabbi Yaakov Yitzchok Horowitz, the Seer of Lublin (1782-1818).

Seer of Lublin – Rabbi Yaakov Yitzchok Horowitz of Lublin (c. 1745-1815). A leading Polish Chasidic Rebbe of the third and fourth generation of the movement. First, a disciple of the Maggid of Mezritch, and then, of Rabbi Elimelech of Lizhensk.

Vilna Gaon – Rabbi Eliyahu of Vilna, Lithuania (1720-1797). One of the greatest Talmudic scholars of the last five hundred years. He was the leader of *misnagdic* (non-hasidic) Jewry, and one of the first opponents of the nascent Chasidic movement.

Notes and Sources

✒ An Invocation

I wrote this for a collection of invocations published in honor of the year 2000. In many ways, it captures the essence of my approach to life, teaching and *avodas Hashem*.

✒ The Soul of Community

This article first appeared in *Parabola* magazine, 17:1 (Winter 1992), in an issue on the theme of "Solitude and Community."

6 – **In an ideal community, each person's place would be so clearly defined as to make him indispensable**: See R. Tzadok HaKohen of Lublin, *Dover Tzedek* §5.

6 – **Solitude holds the promise of such complete and utter commitment to God**: R. Yosef Yitzchok Schneersohn, *Likkutei Dibburim*, trans. Uri Kaploun, vol. 1. (New York: Kehot, 1987) 299–307.

6 – **Abraham was one**: See the introduction to *Likutey Moharan*, part II.

7 – **The head of the community is its leaders**: See R. Moshe Chaim Ephraim of Sidilkov, *Degel Machaneh Ephraim, Shelach*, s.v. "*Od yirmoz*"; *Matos*, s.v. "*Avdeicha*"; *Arvei Nachal, Nasa*; R. Shneur Zalman of Liadi, *Likutey Amarim-Tanya*, chap. 16.

7 – **feet, its financial supporters**: Rabbi Nachman of Breslov, *Likutey Moharan* II:81; R. Tzadok HaKohen, *Machshavos Charutz* §17.

7 – **Every single element is necessary, for if even one is missing:** See R. Tzadok HaKohen, *Dover Tzedek* §5, p.6.

7 – **Kabbalah understands the soul to be a portion of God Himself:** *Degel Machaneh Ephraim*, Vayishlach, s.v. "*Vayishlach*"; *No'am Elimelech*, Kedoshim, s.v. "*Al tifnu el ha'elilim*"; *Pri HaAretz*, Ki Sisa, s.v. "*v'zeh ki sisa es rosh*"; *Meor Einayim*, Yisro, s.v. "*Ach kavanos hama'amar*"; *Kedushas Levi*, Rosh Hashanah, s.v. "*Amar Rabbi Akiva ashreichem Yisroel*"; *Sefer HaTanya*, chap. 2; *Avodas Yisroel*, Ki Setze, s.v. "*Ki Setze la'milchama*." See also BT *Berachos* 10a.

7 – **The soul does not need this world, and God must force it to remain in the body:** R. Moshe Chaim Luzzatto, *Derech Hashem*, 1:3:2; 1:4:2

7 – **Chasidic writings often compare the soul to a flame:** *Be'er Mayim Chaim*, Yisro, s.v. "*v'al zeh amar hakasuv, lo sikrevu l'galos ervah*"; ibid., Tetzaveh, s.v. "*u'lezeh amar hakasuv, ve-atah tetzaveh*"; *Shem miShmuel*, 5673, s.v. "*Inyan shesh arei hamiklat*."

7 – **The soul of man is a candle of God, searching out all the chambers of the heart:** Translation based on Ibn Ezra's commentary on this verse.

7 – **Rabbi Nachman of Breslov, went so far as to say that one hour of solitude a day is a religious obligation:** *Likutey Moharan* II:25.

8 – **so that from within the world itself, a new revelation of the unity of the Creator should emerge:** R. Tzadok HaKohen, *Dover Tzedek*, p. 1.

9 – **Kabbalistic writings consider** *Knesset Yisroel*, **the congregation of the People of Israel, as synonymous with the Shechinah:** R. Yoseph Gikatila, *Sha'arei Orah*, sha'ar 1, sefirah 10; idem, *Sha'arei Tzedek*, sha'ar 5; R. Moshe Cordovero, *Pardes Rimonim*, sha'ar 23, chap. 11; R. Yitzchok Luria, *Sha'ar Ma'amarei Rashbi, ma'amarei Sefer HaZohar m'haRav haGadol*, Bereishis; R. Elimelech of Lizhensk, *No'am Elimelech*, parashas emor, s.v. "*yehi tachas imo*": R. Menachem Mendel of Vitebsk, *Pri HaAretz*, parshas Matos-Masai; R. Levi Yitzchok of Berditchev, *Kedushas Levi*, mesechta Avos 2:5; R. Yisroel of

Alexander, *Yismach Yisroel, parashas Behar*, s.v. *"o ye'omar"*; R. Tzadok HaKohen of Lublin, *Likutey Amoraim*, 16; idem., *Machshavos Charutz*, 4.

9 – **a light to the nations:** Isaiah 42:6, 49:6.

9 – **Every single act, performed according to the laws of the Torah, brings about a greater revelation of God in the world:** R. Tzadok HaKohen, *Dover Tzedek*, p. 1a–b.

9 – **Prayer without intention is like a body without a soul:** R. Yitzchok Luria, *Likutey Torah, parashas Ekev*, s.v. *"Kol hamitzvos,"* first found in R. Yitzchok Abarbanel, *Yeshuas Meshicho*, p. 12a

9 – **This, then, is the role of mankind – to lift back up to God that which is furthest away:** R. Moshe Chaim Luzzatto, *Mesilas Yeshorim*, chap. 26.

9 – **The contemplative is to the community what the soul is to the body:** R. Yaakov Yosef of Polnoye, *Toldos Yaakov Yosef*, Introduction 4; R. Chaim Tyrer, *Be'er Mayim Chaim, Titzaveh*, chap. 27; R. Avraham Yehoshua Heshel of Opte, *Ohev Yisroel, Beha'aloscha*, s.v. *"Vaya'as ken Aharon"*; R. Yehuda Aryeh Leib Alter, *Sfas Emes, Vayigash* 5663.

9 – **"When will the Messiah come?" asks the Talmud:** BT *Yevamos* 62a; *Zohar* 1:28b.

10 – **Then there will be no need for solitude, for the whole world will reveal His glory:** *Derech Hashem* 1:3:13; 1:4:2.

11 – **The entire Torah and the entire world:** Translated by Yaacov David Shulman.

✥ Among Breslover Chasidim

This essay originally appeared in Hillel Zeitlin's Yiddish work, *Reb Nachman Bratzlaver: Der Zeyre Fun Podolia* It was translated by Rabbi Dovid Sears and Rabbi Dovid Zeitlin *z"l*, the latter being a descendant of the extended family of Rabbi Hillel.

✥ A New Song

This essay first appeared in Parabola 29:4 (Fall, 1994), on the theme "The Hidden Treasure."

19 – **It's known that the essence of spiritual work is to come to an ever-renewing vision of God**: *Tzidkas HaTzaddik* §227; See *Kedushas Levi, Eicha*, s.v. "hashivenu Hashem eleicha"; ibid., *Ki Savo*, s.v. "Vayidaber Moshe ve-hakohanim halevi'im";

19 – **Kabbalah perceives reality as multidimensional**: See R. Yitzchok Luria, *Etz Chaim, sha'ar* 1, *anaf* 2, p. 12a.

20 – **At the heart of them all is God, the most concealed, the most intimate**: BT *Berachos* 10a: "Just as God fills the whole world, so the soul fills the whole body... Just as God resides in the innermost chamber, so the soul resides in the innermost chamber."

20 – **the angels mistook him for God**: *Midrash Zuta, Koheles* 6:10.

20 – **the fall of man is understood to mean a fall into the physical, from a body of light to "garments of skin"**: *Tikkunei Zohar* 58, p. 92b; R. Shlomo Elyashev, *Sha'arei HaLeshem*, part 1, s5, s.v. "tafkid ha'adam v'avodato"; R. Chaim Vital, *Sefer HaLikutim, Vayeshev*, chap. 48; *Yismach Moshe, Toldos*; R. Shlomo of Radomsk, *Tiferes Shlomo, Devorim*, s.v. "Eleh hadevorim"; R. Nosson of Breslov, *Likutey Halakhot, Pidyon Peter Chamor* 2:10.

20 – **Chasidic texts speak of fallen loves, fallen fears**: *Degel Machaneh Ephraim, Balak*; *Kesser Shem Tov*, part 2, p. 3a; *Likutey Moharan* I:34, I:54, II:77; *Meor Einayim, Lech Lecha, Va'eschanan*.

21 – **Where did He hide it? In the Torah**: *Degel Machaneh Ephraim, Bereishis*.

22 – **Do not stray to another field, my daughter**: See *Likutey Moharan* I:65, where Rabbi Nachman compares Ruth (of whom this verse speaks) to the soul.

22 – **According to the Talmud, in every generation there are thirty-six hidden Tzaddikim**: BT *Succah* 45b. *Tikkunei Zohar* 21, p. 50b; *Ya'aros D'vash*, part 1, *derash* 9 (*hemshech*); *Sfas Emes, Chanukah* 5650.

22 – **I know, but I cannot tell another**: *Sichos HaRan* 1.

22 – **The very word mitzvah is from the grammatical root of the word "to join"**: R. Yeshayahu Horowitz, *Shnei Luchos HaBris, Assarah Ma'amaros, ma'amar* 3 & 4, §47; ibid. *Mesechta Yoma*,

perek Derech Chaim Tochachos Mussar 16; *Degel Machaneh Ephraim, Korach,* s.v. *"v'yesh l'pharesh";* ibid. *Likutim,* s.v. *"mitzvah"; Pri HaAretz, Ekev; Kedushas Levi, Peirush Agados,* on BT *Bechoros* 8b; *Avodas Yisroel,* on *Pirkei Avos* 3:10; *Likutey Halachos, Netilas Yadayim Shacharis* 4:11; *Sfas Emes, Tetzaveh* 5631

23 – A person who studies Torah selflessly becomes like an ever renewing spring: *Pirkei Avos* 6:1.

23 – every detail of creation has the potential for infinite meaning, because the presence of the Infinite God is beneath the surface waiting to be revealed: See *Likutey Moharan* 1:1.

❧ The Power of Prayer

Heard from Rabbi Avraham Stern, *shlit"a,* who heard it from Rabbi Moshe Aharon Stern *zt"l*

❧ At the Center

This first appeared in Parabola, 22:1 (Winter, 1997), on the theme of "Ways of Knowing."

33 – Matters exceedingly deep, beyond the grasp of the average person: *Mishnah Torah, Yesodei HaTorah* 2:10.

34 – In the writings of later commentators: See R. Shmuel Tanchum Rubinstein, *"Rambam l'Am,"* commentary on the *Mishnah Torah* (Jerusalem: Mossad Harav Kook, 1962) loc. cit., vol. 2, p. 12, n. 5.

34 – He is the knower, the known and the act of knowing: See, also, *Guide for the Perplexed,* part 1, chap. 68.

35 – Maimonides writes that before the Fall, Adam and Eve perceived creation in the objective terms of truth and falsehood: *Guide for the Perplexed,* part 1, chap. 2.

35 – The constant desire for "higher" realization can also be an expression of the ego: See Tractate on Ecstasy, by Rabbi Dovber Shneuri, the Mitteler Rebbe of Chabad.

35 – It is said of the revelation at Sinai that God had to force the Israelites to accept the Torah: BT *Shabbos* 88a.

36 – **Life then becomes defined in terms of... the Oneness and Presence of the Divine:** The Baal Shem Tov taught that at the highest spiritual level, all of one's personal concerns are understood as a lack in the Shechinah, which now becomes the focus of a person's prayers. Many of these teachings are collected in *Sefer Baal Shem Tov, Noach* §152, 153, 154, 155, 166. See also, *Meor Einayim, Naso*; *Likutey Amarim*, p. 18c.

36 – **If spiritual practice does not tear down one's conception of the world:** See *Tzidkas HaTzaddik* §140.

36 – **The Torah only lives in one who kills himself over it:** BT *Berachos* 63b; *Shabbos* 83b; Zohar 2:158b, 3:247a, 278a.

⚜ Through a Dark Passage

This essay first appeared in Parabola 21:2 (Summer, 1996), in an issue on the theme of "The Soul."

45 – **It gazes in a light that shines across creation and learns a supernal wisdom:** BT *Niddah* 30b. See also *Yismach Moshe, Acharei Mos*, s.v. "*Es mishpotai ta'asu.*"

45 – **As the soul descends into the world, it becomes fragmented and broken:** See *Likutey Moharan* 1:54,3; *Likutey Halachos, Chezkas Mitaltilim* 2:1, *Mekach u'Memchar* 1:3. See also *Maor VaShemesh, Acharei*, s.v. "*v'nireh*", *Shoftim*, s.v. "*oh.*"

45 – **Chasidic texts explain that elements of a person's soul can be found in all of his belongings:** *Tzidkas HaTzaddik* §86, 91.

45 – **Soul extends even further, beyond one's immediate realm:** Ibid.

56 – **because their life-source is derived from a particular individual, these things will, over time, reenter his domain:** See sources in from *Likutey Moharan* and *Likutey Halachos*, above.

46 – **The Torah is the "blueprint" of creation:** *Bereishis Rabbah* 1:1.

47 – **Within the daily flood of ideas and emotions, fragments of soul can be found:** *Tzidkas HaTzaddik* §91.

47 – **Kabbalah teaches that in the soul's initial descent to this world, the highest sparks invariably fall to the lowest levels:** *Likutey Moharan* 1:56.

Notes and Sources

48 – **In doing so, it can emerge "with great wealth."** See BT *Berachos* 5a: "Three things can only be obtained through suffering: Torah, the Land of Israel, and the World to Come."

48 – **it will be revealed that the darkest moments of history were actually the times that held the greatest light**: See *Likutey Moharan* 1:21.

49 – **Only looking back will we see how God was present in the places He had previously been concealed**: R. Tzadok HaKohen, *Pri Tzaddik, Ki Setze* §7.

✌ The Paper Piano

I wrote this story in the fall of 1991, after hearing a true story about a French woman – a concert pianist – who had been wrongly interned in a Soviet gulag, after moving back to the USSR with her Russian husband. Her husband died early, but she kept her spirit alive for twenty years by playing on a paper piano. After her release, she remained in Russia to play music for the widows and orphans whose families had also suffered. I was moved by the story, and decided to make a Jewish adaptation. It originally appeared in *Bas Ayin*, issue 6, August 1992.

✌ The Milk of Miracles

This first appeared in Parabola 22:4 (Winter, 1997), in an issue on the theme of "Miracles."

63 – **Daniel in the lion's den, the splitting of the Red Sea, the sun standing still over Gibon**: Daniel 6; Exodus 14; Joshua 10.

64 – **Miracles are more important for what they teach than for what they accomplish**: See Ramban on Exodus 13:16.

64 – **The Hebrew word for miracle is *nes*, which also means "a sign"**: See Rashi on Numbers 26:10.

65 – **Do not rely on a miracle**: BT *Pesachim* 64b.

65 – **The fewer miracles the better**: See R. Tzadok HaKohen, *Divrei Sofrim* §5. See, also, Ramban on Genesis 6:19.

65 – **How unfortunate is he that God had to change the order of creation for his sake**: BT *Shabbos* 53b.

66 – **There is a Kabbalistic principle that every spiritual journey must begin with a revelation**: See R. Tzadok HaKohen, *Tzidkas HaTzaddik* §1-2; *Yisroel Kedoshim*, §7, s.v. *"v'zehu habeis shabbatos,"* p. 68; *Likutey Ma'amarim*, §8, s.v. *"v'zehu hakdamet Shabbos l'mikdash,"* p. 111.

66 – **This is like a father teaching his child to walk**: See *Be'er Mayim Chaim, Noach* §12; *Meor Einayim, Ha'azinu*.

67 – **the world cannot exist without miracles**: *Midrash Shochar Tov, Tehilim* 106.

✒ The Maggid's Coin

First appeared in *Bas Ayin*, issue 10, April 1995. It was inspired by a Native American tale I once read about four warriors who went in search of their fortune, and found some magic object upon which they could each make a wish.

70 – **God gives a Tzaddik dominion over Heaven and earth**: This idea is found in many Chasidic *seforim*. For a classic source, see *Bereishis Rabbah* 77:1: "We find that whatever the Holy One will do in the world to come, the Tzaddikim have already done in this world… revive the dead… visit the barren… sweeten the bitter…"

✒ Seeds of Vision

81 – **Everything has a purpose, and this purpose has another purpose**: *Likutey Moharan* 1:18.

82 – **God "wedges the end in the beginning"** *Sefer Yetzirah* 1:6: "Ten emanations without substance. Ten is their measure, for they have no end. He wedges their end in their beginning and their beginning in the end, like a flame bound to a coal."

83 – **This "drop" is the creation in its perfection, as it arose in God's mind**: This is the meaning of Chazal's statement

Notes and Sources

that God originally desired to create the world with *midas hadin*. Heard from R. Mordechai Zilber, *shlit"a*.

- 84 – **God alone can fix the world using broken tools**: Attributed to R. Menachem Mendel of Kotzk.
- 86 – **the greater the vision, the greater the obstacles**: *Likutey Moharan* I:66.

❧ The Midnight Ride

This story actually happened to me, while I was studying at the Boston Kollel in Har Nof, in 1988, although I wrote it in the third person. It appeared in *Bas Ayin*, issue 7, July 1993.

- 95 – **Each individual has his own path**: *Likutey Halachos, Shomer Sochar* 2:10.

❧ Dweller on the Plain

Originally appeared in *Parabola* 20:1 (Summer, 1995), on the theme of "The Stranger."

- 99 – ***Zar* is also the root of the word "border"**: See Exodus 25:11, 24, 25.
- 101 – **God's primary act of creation is the establishment of a border**: This is the concept of *tzimtzum*, discussed numerous times above.
- 101 – **The various names and descriptions of God... are for our sake alone**: See the introduction to *Olat Tamid*, by R. Chaim Vital. See, also, *Likutey Moharan* II:8.
- 103 – **My eyes are on the faithful of the land**: Literally, "My eyes are *in* the faithful of the land"; that is, God gives us His eyes to see with. See *Likutey Moharan* I:51; I:98 and II:40. See, also, *Yerech HaItanim*, by R. Nachman of Tscherin on *Likutey Moharan* I:9.
- 103 – **Do not belittle any person**: *Pirkei Avos* 4:3.

103 – **God is the "place" of the universe:** *Bereishis Rabbah* 68:9; *Nefesh HaChaim*, by R. Chaim of Volozhin, Part 3, chap. 1-3.

104 – **And Moses stepped into the darkness, where God was:** See *Likutey Moharan* 1:115.

The Souvenir

This story originally appeared in Hebrew in *Sichos HaShavuah* #192, August 31, 1990. The English version first appeared in *Bas Ayin*, issue 11, December 1996.

Writing Between the Lines

Originally appeared in Parabola 28:1 (Spring, 2003), on the theme of "Compassion."

117 – **These are the generations of Isaac:** Kabbalistically, the biblical figures all correspond to various *sefiros*. Abraham is the *sefirah* of *Chesed*, Isaac of *Gevurah*. Yet, paradoxically, Abraham gives birth to Isaac, to the aspect of *Gevurah* latent within him. See *Likutey Amarim*, of R. Dov Baer, the Maggid of Mezritch, 1.

117 – **Just as He is gracious and compassionate:** BT *Shabbos* 133b, *Sotah* 14a. See *The Palm Tree of Devorah*, by R. Moshe Cordovero.

117 – **God's whole reason for creating the universe:** *Likutey Moharan* 1:64.

116 – **a person with compassion has no life:** BT *Pesachim* 113b.

118 – **Only a person who is as cruel to his family as a raven:** BT *Eruvin* 22a.

118 – **the ten *sefiros* also correspond to the ten holy Names of God:** See, for instance, Shaul Boiman, *Maftechei Chochmas HaEmes* (Warsaw: 1937) ch. 46.

119 – **"*Ana nafshi ketavit yehavit*":** BT *Shabbos* 105b. See *Likutey Moharan* 1:173.

Notes and Sources

- 119 – beneath each written letter, at the interface of ink and paper: *Likutey Moharan* 1:18.
- 120 – There are three partners in the creation of a child: BT *Kiddushin* 30b.
- 120 – Words that come from the heart: See BT *Berachos* 6b.
- 120 – For no two things can ever unite... unless space is made for something higher to enter between them: See *Ohev Yisroel, Chukas; Sefas Emes, Korach* 5640; *Shem m'Shmuel, Miketz-Chanukah, Rosh Chodesh Teves; Re'eh* 5675. These are based upon the words of the Maggid of Mezritch, who says that the opposing forces of fire and water (expansion and contraction, *Chesed* and *Gevurah*) are united in heaven by means of self-negation to their Divine source.
- 120 – According to Kabbalah, every human being is also a letter: This is an extrapolation of the Zohar's teaching (*Zohar Chadash, Shir HaShirim, ma'amar* 2) that the 600,000 letters in a Sefer Torah correspond to the 600,000 Jewish men who left Egypt; that is, every Jew corresponds to a letter in the Torah scroll.

❧ Black Fire on White Fire

First appeared in *Bas Ayin*, issue 12. It is retold here by my friend, Rabbi Yehoshua Rubin.

❧ The Still Small Voice

Originally appeared in *Bas Ayin*, issue 9, January 1995.

- 133 – that echoes in creation: See *Baal Shem Tov al HaTorah, Bechukosai* §7 and §8; *Tzidkas HaTzaddik* §222.
- 133 – For the purpose of life is to know God: *Zohar* 2:42b.
- 133 – Chasidic writings speak of "fallen loves": See *Meor Einayim, Lech Lecha; Likutey Moharan* 2:5; *Likutey Halachos, Tefillin* 2:1; *Shechitah* 2:7.

134 – In every place, taught Rabbi Nachman of Breslov, even those places where God is hidden: *Likutey Moharan* 1:56.

134 – The Midrash relates that Abraham beheld a lit-up palace: *Bereishis Rabbah* 39:1.

135 – The world is far from God: *Likutey Moharan* II:10.

135 – Open for me a door the size of a pin-hole: *Zohar* 3:95a.

135 – A pin-size hole is enough to let God in: R. Tzadok HaKohen, *Tzidkas HaTzaddik* §152; *Tikanas HaShavim* 15.

135 – only such a powerful revelation can completely detach the seeker: See *Tzidkas HaTzaddik* §1 and §143.

136 – Beginning practitioners can be recognized: See *Noam Elimelech, parashas Chayei Sarah*; *Ohev Yisroel, parashas Massai*; *Maor VaShemesh, Remazim l'Shevi'i shel Pesach*, "v'nireh": "ein chasidus k'techilaso."

137 – When the soul is aroused by the call of God... the shell of ego that surrounds it is also strengthened: See *Tzidkas HaTzaddik* §206, where this entire process is described.

139 – The voice of my Beloved... Behold, He stands behind our wall: See *Sfas Emes, Pesach* 5543; *Parshas HaChodesh* 6657.

139 – He counts the number of stars and calls them all by their names: See *Badmidbar Rabbah* 11:7.

✤ The Troops of God

This is a true story. I was at the Kotel at the time and witnessed the event myself. It first appeared in *Bas Ayin*, issue 4, April 1992.

142 – From the day the Holy Temple was destroyed: BT *Bava Basra* 12b.

✤ Solomon's Dream

Originally appeared in *Parabola* magazine, 26:4 (Winter, 2001), on the theme of "The Heart."

151 – The heart is the king of the body: *Tikuney Zohar*, chapter 13.

Notes and Sources

151 – **The king is the heart of the nation:** See Maimonides, *Mishnah Torah*, Laws of Kings 3:6.

151 – **Stone hearts, and hearts of flesh:** Based upon Exodus 31:6, Psalms 51:19, and Ezekiel 11:19.

151 – **The heart sees, the heart hears:** *Koheles Rabbah* 1:38, based upon the following verses: Ecclesiastes 1:16; 1 Kings 3:9; Ecclesiastes 1:16; 2 Kings 5:26; 1 Samuel 17:32; Psalms 16:9; Lamentations 2:18; Isaiah 40:2; Deuteronomy 15:10; Leviticus 26:41; Isaiah 21:4; 1 Samuel 4:13; Song of Songs 5:2. The Midrash cites thirty-five more examples.

153 – **He Himself is the place of the entire world:** *Likutey Moharan* II:56.

155 – **All kingship on earth is a reflection of the kingship in heaven:** BT *Berachos* 58a.

155 – **There is no king without a people:** *Kad HaKemach, Rosh Hashanah* 70a.

155 – **God withdrew Himself to the sides, in the center of His light, leaving an empty space:** *Otzros Chaim, Sha'ar HaIgulim* I, by Rabbi Chaim Vital, based on the teachings of R. Yitzchok Luria.

155 – **My heart is empty within me:** See *Likutey Moharan* I:49. See also Maimonides, *Mishnah Torah*, Laws of King 2:6, who lists this trait as one of the requirements of a king of Israel.

✧ Standing Beneath the Mountain

Originally appeared in *Parabola*, 29:1 (Spring, 2004), in an issue on the theme of "Marriage."

163 – **The Patriarchs observed all the laws of the Torah:** BT *Yoma* 28b, based on Genesis 26:5: "All this because Abraham obeyed My voice, and kept My charge, My commandments, My statutes, and My laws."

164 – **If you accept My Torah, fine. If not...:** BT *Shabbos* 88a.

164 – **The Torah was given by force:** R. Yitzchok Eisik Yehudah Yechiel Safrin, *Notzer Chesed* (Lemburg: 1856) I. See also *Tzidkas HaTzaddik* §56.

165 – **The purely righteous do not complain about evil:** Rabbi Abraham Isaac Kook, *Arpelei Tohar* (Jerusalem: Machon R. Tzvi Yehuda Kook, 1983) 39.

166 – **If a husband and wife are worthy, the Divine Presence dwells between them:** BT *Sotah* 17a.

⁓ Slim

This story was told to me by Rabbi Chaim Levin, the young man in the episode (the other names have been changed). R. Chaim has worked in anti-missionary and anti-cult activities for many years, although the following incident occurred before he began that line of activity. I first published it in *Bas Ayin*, issue 9, January 1995.

189 – **Chaim... it was worth it:** According to Chaim, Rachel Praeger eventually left her "friends" in Arizona and returned home, where she was lovingly received.

⁓ Song of the Shepherds

Retold from *Rabbi Tzvi Elimelech of Dinov*, p. 166.

⁓ The Temple of Amount

Originally appeared in Parabola 24:3 (Fall, 1999), on the theme of "Number and Symbol."

185 – **From the 'I am' of flesh and blood:** *Bereishis Rabbah* 90:2

188 – **The system of the *mitzvos* [commandments] constitutes the design for a coherent harmony:** Rabbi Adin Steinsaltz, *The Thirteen Petaled Rose* (Northvale, NJ: Aronson, 1992).

189 – **Let a person study Torah even for self-centered reasons:** BT *Pesachim* 50b.

191 – **Who can bring the pure out of the impure?:** *Bamidbar Rabbah* 19:1.

Notes and Sources

✒ The Untouched Oil

This original story first appeared in *Chosen Tales: Stories Told by Jewish Storytellers*, Peninnah Schram (ed.), Aronson Pub., 1995. It was inspired by a Liberian folktale that I heard from Peninnah, which she also adapted into a Jewish story called "The Golden Watch," which appears in her book *Jewish Stories One Generation Tells Another* (Northvale, NJ: Aronson, 1992) 457-464.

✒ Responsibility

201 – **freedom was inscribed on the tablets:** This is not a literal translation of the verse, but one based upon the reading of the Sages in *Pirkei Avos* (6:2): "Do not read the word as *charus* (inscribed) but as *cherus* (freedom), for the only free person is one who studies Torah."

✒ The Age of Tikkun

Originally appeared in Parabola 23:1 (Spring, 1998), in an issue on the theme of "Millennium."

203 – **The *mitzvos* were only given to purify the world:** *Bereishis Rabbah* 44:1.

204 – **when God first formed the universe, He left it incomplete:** See *Pirkei d'Rebbi Eliezer*, chap. 3.

204 – **There is a direct relationship between the act of *tikkun* and the movement from slavery to freedom:** See R. Tzadok HaKohen, *Pri Tzaddik, Tu b'Shevat* §1; R. Nosson, *Likutey Halachot, Tzitzit* 3:14; *Birchas HaShachar* 3:17; *Pesach* 2:1, among many other places.

205 – **A slave must be fed and clothed well:** BT *Kiddushin* 20a. See, also, Exodus 21:26-27.

206 – **When all the illusions of the world have finally been exhausted:** R. Tzadok HaKohen, *Risisei Leilah*, p. 142.

207 – **God showed him all the generations that would emerge from him:** *Shemos Rabbah* 40:3.

207 – Even the beggar on the street must give charity: *Shulchan Aruch, Yoreh Deah* 248:1.
208 – When God created Adam, He took him around the Garden of Eden: *Koheles Rabbah* 7:13.

ಆ A Single Glance

First appeared in *Sichos HaShavuah* #556, Aug. 29, 1997. My version appeared in *Bas Ayin*, issue 13, April 1998.

ಆ

> This is the whole point that our Sages sought to convey to us through their writings. To stand us on that threshold, as small as the eye of a needle, which is the recognition that everything comes from God, blessed be He. Then God Himself opens the chambers of our hearts, so that we may know and understand with depth and certainty how everything *is* from God. And that all the wise men and leaders of past generations are also the leaders of our generation, teaching and enlightening us, as well.
>
> Because, you see, we come from them, and each generation contains within it all subsequent generations, just as the soul of the son exists potentially within the soul of the father. Our present generation was itself included within all the generations from Moses until today. Therefore, our Sages wrote down their wisdom in books to aid those coming after them, for all of them were truly included in their own generation and their own souls.
>
> R. Tzadok HaKohen of Lublin
> *Likutey Mamorim* 46a

www.ingramcontent.com/pod-product-compliance
Lightning Source LLC
Chambersburg PA
CBHW051750040426
42446CB00007B/301